THE TEXAS POST OFFICE MURALS

Number Fourteen:
Joe and Betty Moore Texas Art Series

In Memoriam
Joe Hiram Moore, 1917–2003

THE TEXAS
POST OFFICE MURALS

Art for the People

Philip Parisi

TEXAS A&M UNIVERSITY PRESS ✉ COLLEGE STATION

The paper used in this book meets the minimum requirements
of the American National Standard for Permanence
of Paper for Printed Library Materials, z39.48-1984.
Binding materials have been chosen for durability.

Library of Congress Cataloging-in-Publication Data

Parisi, Philip, 1945–
The Texas Post Office murals : art for the people / Philip Parisi. — 1st ed.
p. cm. — (Joe and Betty Moore Texas art series ; no. 14)
Includes bibliographical references.
ISBN 1-58544-231-3 (cloth : alk. paper)
1. Mural painting and decoration, American — Texas — History — 20th century. 2. Post office buildings — Texas.
3. United States. Federal Works Agency. Section of Fine Arts. I. Texas. Post Office Dept. II. Title. III. Series.
ND2635.T4 P37 2003
751.7'3'0976409041 — dc21
2003003567

For my wife, Sue Shapiro

CONTENTS

PREFACE

Texas post office murals first captured my attention in 1989 while I was working as an editor for the Texas Historical Commission. I was researching another topic and accidentally discovered a collection of 35mm color slides stored in the bottom drawer of a filing cabinet. Despite the small size and somewhat blurry resolution of the slide images—copies of copies—the scenes' energy and vigor impressed me. The earthy style depicted Texas history and culture simply and directly. The images created a kaleidoscope of Texas' past—Spanish conquistadors, cowboys branding cattle on the range, a stampede of longhorns terrified by a thunderstorm, and pioneer families with expectant gleams in their eyes as they arrived by covered wagon on the Texas frontier. Several slides featured montages that combined scenes of daily life, work, and local industries such as oil, mining, fishing, and lumber manufacturing. Who painted these pictures and why? Where were the original artworks located?

I discovered that the slide images were of murals, or wall paintings, placed in various Texas post offices during the Great Depression. The post office murals represented a unique federal art patronage program that brought art to the people throughout the United States—part of President Franklin D. Roosevelt's New Deal. I was disappointed to learn that now, some fifty years after they first appeared, the artworks were endangered. Several of them had been destroyed or reported missing; others were neglected and deteriorating. The THC's collection of slides belonged to an audiovisual program produced in the early 1980s as part of a mural survey.[1] The program was available for public loan and checked out occasionally by a few teachers, but the mural images remained generally out of the public eye.

My first reactions as a journalist and preservationist was to bring these compelling images to greater public attention—to revive the memory of them and encourage their preservation. I subsequently wrote a feature article about the Texas post office murals for the THC's newsletter and included black-and-white reproductions of three murals. The article drew a flood of letters and telephone calls from enthusiastic readers, some of whom wanted to express how much the murals had meant to them as children when they stopped at the post office with their parents. Many people wanted to know something more about the murals in their community and about other murals in Texas. Some people said that they had known of the murals but were surprised to learn of their number and variety.

The brisk public response to the newsletter article encouraged me to assemble a traveling exhibit of enlarged mural photos. At about the same time the newsletter article had appeared, *Texas Monthly* magazine featured a photo essay of a few of the murals recently taken by Austin photographer Wyatt McSpadden.[2] Here were the high-quality images I sought for the THC exhibit. I was able to secure several of McSpadden's photographs, with the support of the Texas Historical Commission and a grant from the Texas Committee for the Humanities, and have them made into large-format prints that comprised the core number of the exhibit's two dozen images. In late 1990, after its initial showing in Austin's Capitol rotunda, the exhibit went on the road. Meanwhile, the *Dallas Morning News* published an article I had written about the murals.[3] Letters and phone calls concerning the exhibit and the newspaper article again bombarded THC headquarters. The exhibit's success surpassed all expectations. For the next nine years the exhibit traveled to scores of schools, post offices, and museums across the state, always drawing praises.

Despite the exhibit's popularity, it represented less than one-third of all the Texas post office murals and included only a brief background narrative. Many of the most interesting murals were necessarily omitted, and fascinating stories that surrounded their creation remained hidden. To better understand and appreciate the murals, people needed a more complete visual record and a narrative account of these cultural treasures.

Not everyone can travel to find the dozens of post office murals in every corner of Texas. Moreover, many of the murals are difficult to see in situ, because they are usually located high on the lobby wall above the postmaster's door. Post office additions of low-suspended light fixtures, air-conditioning ducts, and lobby partitions in many cases obstruct clear views of the murals.

This book, in effect, brings the murals down from the walls, making them available for the first time all in one place. Although spread throughout the sections of this book, all images for a given city or by a given artist may be located by using the book's index.

The clarity of McSpadden's photographs reveals details in the murals that would otherwise be missed. Because some of the murals have been destroyed or lost, we are fortunate that the Section of Fine Arts, the federal agency that administered the post office mural program, required artists to submit large-format photographs of their completed murals. Some of these black-and-white images—reproduced here from negatives housed at the Still Pictures Branch of the National Archives in College Park, Maryland—represent the now-destroyed or missing murals. Color photos of two murals are included from the Smithsonian American Art Museum, Smithsonian Institution, in Washington, D.C., where the murals are in storage.

ACKNOWLEDGMENTS

My appreciation goes to the Texas Historical Commission for its support and to individual members of its staff for allowing me the time and resources to pursue this project. I also appreciate the support of the Brown Foundation of Houston, which provided me a grant to complete research at the National Archives in Washington, D.C., and to commission some of the book's photography. The Texas Committee for the Humanities initially funded the mural exhibit. I wish to thank the staffs of the U.S. Postal Service Federal Preservation Office and the General Services Administration Fort Worth region and headquarters in Washington, D.C., for their assistance securing mural survey information. Finally, I thank all those who have helped bring the publication of this book to fruition.

THE TEXAS POST OFFICE MURALS

THE STORY OF
TEXAS POST OFFICE MURALS

Post office murals are the people's art. They portray the everyday lives, hopes, and aspirations of Americans. The murals sparkle with life and scenes taken from history, folklore, heroes, and regional landscapes. Yet, casual observers who happen upon the artworks may find them puzzling anachronisms—or marvelous surprises. Few people—even post office employees—can offer information about the origin or purpose of the murals or the particular images at that specific site. Visitors leave with little more than a series of unanswered questions.

In Texas, artists created 106 artworks for sixty-nine post offices and federal buildings.[1] The general subject matter of some of the murals may seem obvious, but their historical and narrative meaning often remains shrouded. When artists originally installed the murals, descriptive guides about each mural and about the artists were hung in the post office lobby. These information sheets disappeared long ago. Many mural titles, which could help viewers interpret what they see, remain unknown or unpublicized. Yet a title itself, such as "San Antonio's Importance in Texas History," may do little to explain a complex series of historical events portrayed in the sixteen panels of that mural sequence. Located high above the archways in the foyer of the federal courthouse and post office in San Antonio, the mural presents a pageant of images of Indians, pioneers, the Alamo (which is located across the street), and longhorns. Viewers, however, are left to their own resources to identify and sort out the precise historical events and characters in the panels. This volume will enable viewers to understand Texas post office murals visually and historically. It will provide vital information concerning both the artists' and the federal government's purposes.

Painted by some of the most promising and well-known artists of the 1930s, these public artworks present a broad range of regional subjects. The Texas post office murals portray Texans' values embodied in such characters as the revered Indian chief Quanah Parker, cowboys, the bandit and folk hero Sam Bass, Texas Rangers, and historical figures Davy Crockett and Sam Houston. Several murals even focus on Texas longhorns, important symbols of Texas' historical identity.

Viewers who have little or no previous exposure to art can appreciate the post office murals' simple, direct style. Like all art, the post office murals provide clues about the times in which they were created. The murals reflect the efforts of a country trying to recapture a vision of its greatness, a vision that had been reduced to a sputtering flame as the effects of the Great Depression swept across the country. After the collapse of the stock market in 1929 and the disintegration of such seemingly unshakable institutions as the banking system, many Americans succumbed to crippling fear and feelings of despair. The Roosevelt administration designed the New Deal program to provide tangible relief to Americans. Administrators intended to boost Americans' self-confidence and inspire citizens to rebuild their lives and, ultimately, the country's economy.

In attempts to reverse the country's depression-related economic and social woes, the Roosevelt administration initiated numerous public work and relief projects under an array of individual programs.[2] One group of unem-

"San Antonio's Importance in Texas History: Santa Anna before Sam Houston" by Howard Cook. Photo by Wyatt McSpadden.

ployed people, however, fell outside the net of government assistance. In 1933, artist George Biddle urged his old school friend President Franklin D. Roosevelt to employ artists for weekly wages to assist them economically and, secondarily, to beautify the walls of public buildings with positive images of American life and history. The artworks would support New Deal objectives by bringing powerful, visual messages of hope to the people.[3] Biddle's letter cited the 1920s Mexican mural renaissance as an example of how government-sponsored art could inspire public pride. Mexican artists such as Diego Rivera, José Clemente Orozco, and David Alfaro Siqueiros had depicted important national themes on the walls of Mexico's public buildings.[4] In turn, American artists, Biddle wrote, "would be contributing to and expressing in living monuments the social ideals that you are struggling to achieve. And I am convinced that our mural art with a little impetus can soon result, for the first time in our history, in a vital national expression."[5]

President Roosevelt accepted Biddle's idea to sponsor public art murals in the Mexican mural tradition. When skeptics questioned federal support of artists, Harry Hopkins, the director of both the Works Progress Administration and the Civil Works Administration, defended the project to employ artists: "Hell! They've got to eat just like other people."[6]

Roosevelt called upon Edward Bruce, an international monetary expert and official with the U.S. Treasury Department, to organize a public art program. Bruce, himself an accomplished painter, enthusiastically embraced the challenge. In 1933, under his direction, the U.S. Treasury Department launched a six-month pilot program called the Public Works of Art Project. PWAP administrators operated under the fundamental assumption that beauty could function as an anodyne for the sense of despair that seemed to pervade the country. Bruce and others believed that creating a demand for beauty would have long-ranging effects: under this impetus, slums would eventually disappear, and beauty would replace ugliness. As Bruce observed, "There is a desire for beauty, a reaction against the ugliness that surrounds us, a wish to fill one's time with new interests, a hope to find an outlet for the creative spirit."[7]

Meanwhile, administrators debated where to place the artworks. In 1933, an ambitious public building program made available nearly $145 million in public funds for the construction of 233 federal buildings, hospitals, courthouses, executive buildings, schools, libraries, post offices, and other public structures around the country.[8] Under PWAP one percent of the building cost normally reserved for structure decoration was to be used to pay artists to create murals for designated structures. Thus, more than $1 million from the Civil Works Administration budget was initially allocated for artworks. By June, 1934, when PWAP ended, about 15,660 works of art, including 700 murals by some 3,750 artists were displayed nationwide.[9] Armed with such success, PWAP staff convinced the federal government in October, 1934, to extend the program by creating the Section of Painting and Sculpture (renamed the Section of Fine Arts 1938–43), to be administered by the U.S. Treasury Department. Bruce continued as the Section's director.

Like PWAP, the Section was not intended primarily as a relief program, although it was a boon to participating artists. Compared with projects sponsored by the WPA and other art programs, the goal of the Section of Fine Arts was to procure higher-quality art.[10] The Section would place original works of art in new *post offices* only. PWAP had sponsored art for a variety of public buildings. The Section focused on reaching as many people as possible across the country. What better place to accomplish this goal than to install murals in local post offices, which often doubled as social centers where people met and interacted daily? As post office patrons regularly waited in line to purchase stamps or mail a package, they would be able to see and dwell on the mural images and reflect on local history and folklore. Art in public buildings had traditionally featured themes from classical mythology—subjects that seemed remote from current, more pressing concerns in the lives of Americans. New post office mural art would instead address subjects to which Americans could relate. Section administrators stressed that mural subject matter was to follow the American Scene style associated with Thomas Hart Benton and others who had been inspired by Diego Rivera and other Mexican muralists.[11] American Scene sprang from a desire to return to America's roots. For post office murals, this meant featuring activities of daily rural and city life and regional, historical subjects.[12]

The Section of Fine Arts' mission resembled that of PWAP, which selected artists on the basis of artistic merit. Both programs sought to develop a uniquely American art and raise the level of American culture. Funding arrangements differed between the two programs, however. Whereas PWAP and other federal relief programs provided relief to artists through hourly wages, the Section of Fine Arts paid for high-quality art through contracts won in open competitions. The Section divided the country into sixteen regions and sponsored a series of regional and national competitions. It invited artists to submit their designs anonymously to a citizen committee, usually composed of artists, critics, and at least one architect. The citizen committees prescreened the unsigned works, chose the best, and sent the numbered, color sketches along with winning artists' names in sealed envelopes to the Section of Fine Arts in Washington for final judging. The anonymity of artists in the selection process gave all competing artists, regardless of their ethnicity or gender, a fair opportunity (at least in theory) to land a contract. Section administrators frequently offered competing artists whose works won honorable mention commissions to create murals for smaller post offices, although local citizens also had a say in determining the art to be placed in their community. As a result, the Section of Fine Arts stood out from other New Deal art programs, not only because of the competition for commissions that ensured work of the highest quality possible but also because of the democratic nature of the selection process.

Howard Cook sitting before San Antonio mural. Courtesy *San Antonio Light* Collection, Institute of Texan Cultures, San Antonio, Texas.

McVey relief of Sam Houston's San Jacinto report. Courtesy National Archives, Section of Fine Arts, Public Building Administration.

Because artists and administrators involved with the Section of Fine Arts wanted to see federal art patronage continue permanently, officials tried not to allow controversies to jeopardize the program. Nevertheless, the Section of Fine Arts drew occasional fire. As the Dallas gallery entry recounts, the Section initially awarded the commission for the Dallas Parcel Post Building to two artists, not from Texas, but from California. About a dozen Dallas artists, led by Jerry Bywaters and Alexandre Hogue, cried foul. A heated debate ensued, resulting in a showdown with the Section and some bitter feelings.

The Section of Fine Arts records — located in the National Archives — while somewhat sparse, are among the most intact of records of the federal arts programs. They contain correspondence among artists, government officials, postal officials, and citizens, as well as federal press releases and local newspaper articles that were circulated at the time of the murals' creation. These sources have provided much of the material needed to tell the story of the Texas post office murals. The gallery entries necessarily reflect the abundance or paucity of information available. A few of the more articulate artists, such as Tom Lea and Jerry Bywaters, corresponded frequently and in great detail with federal officials about their work. In other cases, the artists were pen-shy.

Yet even the most laconic artists could sometimes offer insights into the creative process and other significant details. Some murals caused unusual public attention because of their contentious subject matter or polarizing issues surrounding their creation. Because the actual words of the artists and Section leaders bring a unique sense of immediacy, the gallery entries contain many direct quotations from these original sources. The comments will undoubtedly enrich the viewers' experience and understanding of the murals themselves.

The term "mural" comes from the Latin word *murus*, meaning wall. Thus, murals are artworks that appear on walls. Although some of the Section of Fine Arts murals were relief sculptures of carved wood (Hereford, Waco), molded stone (Bryan, Houston, Littlefield), or plaster (Electra), most Texas murals were paintings executed in oil on canvas. Artists usually created their murals in their studios and later traveled to glue or hang them on the post office walls. Some murals, however, were done in fresco, that is, a method by which artists applied pigment directly to wet plaster. The Italian Renaissance masters—Fra Angelico, Piero della Francesca, and, later, Michelangelo—perfected this method, which Mexican muralists revived in the 1920s. Murals painted on dry plaster and called fresco secco (Baytown, Hamilton) were generally not as resilient as those done in true fresco.

Few of the post office mural artists were trained as muralists. Many of them received coaching from Section of Fine Arts administrators, some of whom were artists themselves. The Section required contracted muralists to create clear and simple designs that average people, unschooled in art or art history, could understand. The murals had to be realistic and include familiar symbols of the people's lives so that they could easily believe in the authenticity of the images. The murals' location — later designated to be above the postmaster's door — challenged the artists technically. The space was narrow, with a relatively shallow vertical and a very broad horizontal dimension. In an effort to compensate for such an awkward space, many artists incorporated the postmaster's door into the painting, extending the work down slightly along ei-

"Cattle" by Allie Tennant in Electra post office. Photo by Philip Parisi.

ther side of the door frame. This technique better allowed artists to add some perspective to their paintings.

Although artists were free to compete for mural commissions, once an artist accepted a government contract, the art to be produced became a matter for negotiation. As might be expected in patron-supported art, artistic freedom sometimes yielded to the taste of federal officials who ran the program. The Section's chief administrator, Edward Rowan, in his correspondence with artists, repeatedly stressed that the Section of Fine Arts did not want to influence the artists' decisions unduly.[13] Nevertheless, as the correspondence shows, the Section did not hesitate to exercise its influence on mural style, subject, and point of view. Rowan guided artists through each phase of the work — preliminary sketch to final product — asking them to correct awkwardly drawn elements and alter their compositions to conform to the Section's esthetic. For example, when Section officials repeatedly forced Bernard Zakheim to change the facial features of a particularly repulsive figure in his Rusk post office mural, a prominent community leader wrote to Rowan in Zakheim's defense. He argued emphatically that Zakheim's mural character was an accurate likeness of a popular local figure! The Section refused to compromise.

Similarly, artists were strongly urged to seek local opinion when choosing subject matter. In Amarillo, the local newspaper invited citizens to suggest to the artist what they wanted included in their new mural. The article opened a floodgate of candid responses, revealing people's views of themselves as well as their idyllic visions for the future of their region. The Section wished to avoid potentially offensive or distasteful subjects, however, even if the people's desires — most often communicated through the postmaster — had to be disregarded. When the Giddings postmaster wanted to see the interior workings of the local poultry processing plant immortalized in the post office mural, the Section insisted on a cleaner subject. In some cases, as the Kenedy gallery entry documents, civic leaders emphasized that certain aspects of a community's past were off limits, and both artist and Section administrators ultimately respected their wishes.

About a third of Texas post office murals portray historical subjects, and numerous others contain history as an element in a larger context. Artists' depiction of positive historical subjects reminded people of better times. The murals deemphasized the uncertain present, that is, the difficult times brought on by the depression.[14] By implying that the era was part of a continuum, historical murals suggested that Americans would overcome existing challenges. History thus fulfilled the psychological need for stability and continuity.[15] (See especially gallery entries for

"Music of the Plains" by Xavier Gonzalez in Kilgore post office. Photo by Wyatt McSpadden.

Amarillo, Brady, Dallas, Kilgore, and Mart.) Themes of labor were closely allied to historical themes. In 1933, about 13 million people were out of work nationally.[16] Murals showing people at work — especially in local industries — provided subtle encouragement to Americans who viewed them.[17] Texas work murals feature industries specific to the region, including cotton, oil exploration, and ranching. These subjects often were combined with symbols of progress, such as manufacturing or agricultural machinery and new methods of transportation.

Folklore and local legend also served as popular mural subjects. Tom Lea based his Odessa post office mural, "Stampede," on a dramatic moment in a famous cowboy ballad with which West Texans may have easily identified.[18] One corner of the Eastland post office mural includes the depiction of a horned lizard, which casual observers may easily overlook or dismiss. But area residents readily identify the lizard as "Ol' Rip," the much-beloved subject of a fantastic legend that thrives today among Eastland residents. Other muralists also included strategic references to local culture, tradition, or landscape.

The importance of authenticity emerges as a constant refrain in the accounts of the creation of Texas post office murals. As many of the gallery entries document, Texans demanded that their community's past be accurately and realistically represented in their post office mural. Section administrators had the foresight to accommodate this requirement, and they generally held the artists accountable for avoiding abstract treatments and for ironing out awkward passages in their murals. Artists such as Tom Lea, however, needed no encouragement to produce factually accurate treatments. His correspondence with Rowan reveals a passion for authenticity that was integral to his artistic style, and he went to extraordinary lengths to ensure conformity to facts. (See El Paso gallery entry.)

Although most artists happily accepted their contracts and commissions, a few grumbled about the terms and esthetic demands of the Section. Outspoken Dallas artist Alexandre Hogue, for example, took Washington to task for meddling in his work. (See Graham gallery entry.) Of course, the most cogent incentive for artists to comply with Section demands to modify their style or subject was receiving a paycheck. The Section's three-stage payment structure guaranteed its complete control over each mural. The Section of Fine Arts issued a check after approving each stage of the work. Thus, artists dutifully implemented Section administrators' suggestions in order to receive the next installment of their payment.

Despite pecuniary compensation from mural commissions, the experience of working for the federal government could prove distressing. Some artists noted the meager size of the paychecks (between $600 and $900, though sometimes more, depending on the post office construction cost), as well as their untimely arrival. Needy

Part of "Pass of the North" mural by Tom Lea in El Paso post office. Photo by Wyatt McSpadden.

artists seldom anticipated the potential frustrations of dealing with federal bureaucracy on the issue of payment. Moreover, artists were expected to use their own money to buy top-quality, expensive canvas and materials, hire assistants if necessary, and often travel long distances to the mural site. Then, after they had worked weeks and months on a mural, sometimes far from home, months more might pass before they received their payment. When installment checks were overdue, and no explanations were forthcoming, artists grew increasingly frantic. Their written requests to the Section to speed up payment often began discreetly with indirect, tactful hints. As delays stretched into months, artists' diplomatic hints to hurry things along gradually became outright pleas. If, as sometimes happened, the polite requests still went unheeded, the artists resorted to sardonic humor and finally to cries of desperation. After numerous requests for payment, for example, artist William McVey complained that he was "getting weary of beans twice a day!" Emil Bisttram's finances became so depleted that he reported he could not proceed with the mural in Ranger because he could not afford to buy art materials.[19] "This business of being broke," he wrote to Rowan, "one gets used to but it is inconvenient as well as embarrassing when one has obligations elsewhere."[20] Tom Lea tactfully expressed his desperation in the tone of a humble, understated plea: "Please forgive me for making any reference to my financial troubles — but . . . my present situation gives me great worry."[21]

Theodore Van Soelen at first couched his need for payment in an amusing health metaphor: "Like all artists," he confessed, "and most other people, my bank account is usually in a deplorably anemic condition. A small check now and then revives it and sends my financial corpuscles swirling around."[22] Six months later, his letters revealed more desperation, as the artist switched metaphors and melodramatically compared his financial state to a German war tactic. "If you can push my final check along on that contract — before Christmas — the undersigned will be able to face the bills bravely — otherwise I am blitzkrieged."[23] Finally, Van Soelen issued a bald plea in current American idiom for expediting his check: "I am worried stiff about my bills. They have me absolutely backed to the wall. Is there any way my second payment (and the first) can be hustled along?"[24] Rowan managed to grease the bureaucratic wheels a bit, and payment finally arrived, but not before Van Soelen was forced to cash in an insurance policy to finance a trip to another mural job![25]

The gallery entries present evidence of residents' immediate reactions to their new murals and first-hand insight into the people and the times. Texans were sometimes flattered to have "real artists" take a detailed interest in them and in representing their lives in art. Even so, many regarded artists with suspicion. The stereotype of Bohemian artists — social outcasts given to extremes of be-

Howard Cook working on preliminary sketches for San Antonio mural. Courtesy *San Antonio Light* Collection, Institute of Texan Cultures, San Antonio, Texas.

havior and loose moral conduct — dampened artists' receptions in some rural communities. But, as each party discovered something about the other, mutual understanding usually followed. Some artists kept journals of spontaneous comments they overheard as they worked in public, while either painting fresco murals on location or installing their murals prepared in other media. Spectators' reactions ranged from astonishment to bemused speculation to feelings of disgust. Newspaper accounts also offer insightful information about the local population's immediate reception of artists and their art. Occasionally, as in Brownfield, a special bond even developed between the artist and the townspeople, despite signs of a shaky beginning.

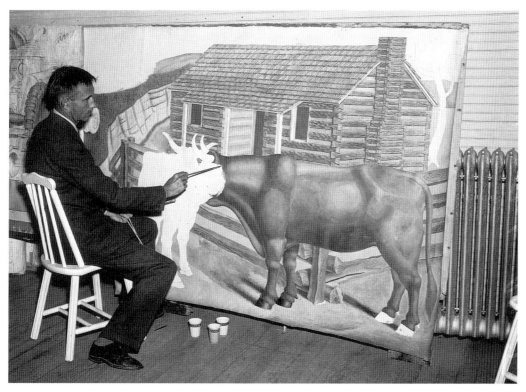

Thomas M. Stell, Jr., working on mural for Longview post office. Courtesy *San Antonio Light* Collection, Institute of Texan Cultures, San Antonio, Texas.

As post offices continue to remodel old facilities or abandon their outdated buildings for newer structures, the fate of the murals becomes increasingly uncertain. As of 2003, seven Texas post office murals already have been lost, destroyed, or have simply vanished without explanation. Some murals have fallen victim to "progress." In Livingston, for example, where the old post office is now being used as the city police station, the two murals were all but destroyed during 1997 building renovations, when they were peeled from the wall. Officials seldom give the public advance notice of such ill-conceived plans. Furthermore, laws for the treatment of murals are sketchy. Post office murals are federal property and — theoretically, at least — they should not be removed or altered without

permission. In practice, however, murals have frequently been subjected to sudden whim. Under such circumstances, concerned citizens may be powerless to stop the destruction. The Henderson post office mural was painted over in 1956 during remodeling. A resident recalled: "After the new and present post office was built, the older building was sold and the inside walls painted over. I could have cried. . . . Can a mural painted on plaster and later painted over be preserved?"[26] Two post office murals (in Alice and Edinburg) were carefully removed at the time of post office demolitions, and, although they are safe in storage at the Smithsonian American Art Museum, they remain out of public view.

Murals also are lost through neglect. Over the years,

Francis S. Ankrom, architect, stands beside his recently completed mural, "Strays," that he painted for the Canyon post office. Courtesy *San Antonio Light* Collection, Institute of Texan Cultures, San Antonio, Texas.

"Loading Cattle" by Otis Dozier as seen on the walls of the Fredricksburg post office. Photo by Philip Parisi.

Seymour post office with view of Tom Lea's "Comanches." Photo by Matt Gwinn.

lack of public awareness or understanding about them has undoubtedly contributed to their mistreatment and, in some cases, their demise. Several murals in need of attention languish in buildings left vacant (Decatur) or used for storage (Lamesa). After years of neglect, some of the murals, such as the one at La Grange, are in need of restoration. To their credit, the U.S. Postal Service, as well as the General Services Administration, have had several murals cleaned and restored.[27] Still other scenes have been professionally cleaned and preserved through the efforts of concerned citizens who have raised the required funds. Other murals, however, may be beyond restoration, such as the faded fresco at the Baytown post office (now a museum), or the Hamilton post office mural, which, despite efforts to stabilize it, continues to flake off the wall.

This volume provides basic knowledge about the murals—their content, their historical context, their artistic symbolism, the artists' intentions, and the reactions of the people for whom the artworks were originally meant. Beneath the surface of each Texas post office mural lies a fascinating story. The entries in this book will present these stories and allow viewers to understand and enjoy the murals more thoroughly. Each mural entry supplies the mural's identity, including title, artist, size, and medium, together with the background information from the artists' correspondence and other sources.

The images presented in this book capture the vitality and compelling energy of Texas post office murals and make the murals accessible to the people. There is much to be said for having a first-hand viewing experience, and this book may encourage people to visit as many mural sites as they possibly can. The book brings together the murals' context and dynamic imagery to foster a new understanding and enjoyment of the murals, reframe them, and encourage people to restore and preserve a historic and artistic legacy.

Plate 1. Corpus Christi, "The Sea: Port Activities" (detail) by Howard Cook (1941).

Plate 2. Decatur, "Texas Plains" by Ray Strong (1939).

Plate 3. Quanah, "The Naming of Quanah" (detail) by Jerry Bywaters (1938).

Plate 4. Seymour, "Comanches" by Tom Lea (1942).

HES

Plate 5. Borger, "Big City News" by José Aceves (1939).

Plate 6. Canyon, "Strays" by Francis Ankrom (1938).

Plate 7. Hereford, "On the Range" by Enid Bell (1941).

Plate 8. El Paso, "Coronado's Exploration Party in the Palo Duro Canyon" (detail) by Tom Lea (1938).

Plate 9. Amarillo, "Cattle Branding" by Julius Woeltz (1941).

Plate 10. Amarillo, "Disk Harrow" by Julius Woeltz (1941).

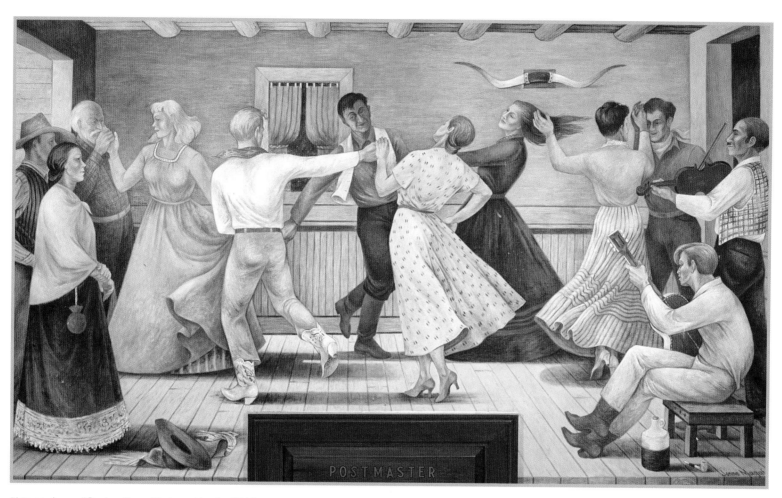

Plate 11. Anson, "Cowboy Dance" by Jenne Magafan (1941).

Plate 12. Arlington, "Gathering Pecans" by Otis Dozier (1941).

Plate 13. Brownfield, "Ranchers of the Panhandle Fighting Prairie Fire with Skinned Steer" (detail) by Frank Mechau (1940).

Plate 14. Dallas, "Pioneer Home Builders" (detail) by Peter Hurd (1940).

Plate 15. Dallas, "Airmail over Texas" by Peter Hurd (1940).

Plate 16. El Paso, "Pass of the North" by Tom Lea (1938).

Plate 17. Fort Worth,
"Flags over Texas"
by Frank Mechau (1940).

Plate 18. Farmersville, "Soil Conservation
in Collin County" by Jerry Bywaters (1941).

Plate 19. Eastland, "Indian Buffalo Hunt" by Suzanne Scheuer (1939).

Plate 20. Gatesville, "Off to Northern Markets" by Joe DeYong (1939).

Plate 21. Giddings, "Cowboys Receiving the Mail" by Otis Dozier (1939).

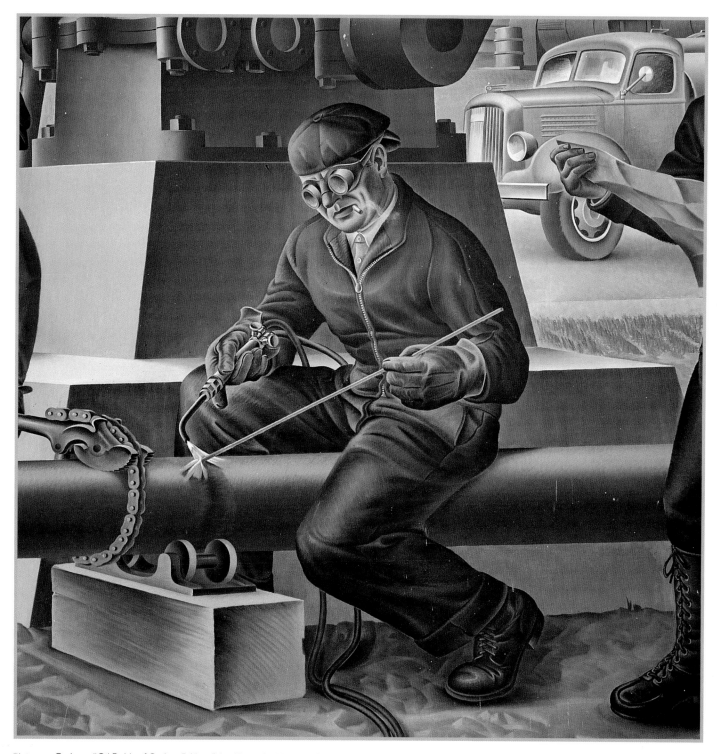

Plate 22. Graham, "Oil Fields of Graham" (detail) by Alexandre Hogue (1939).

Plate 23. Hamilton, "Texas Rangers in Camp" by Ward Lockwood (1942).

Plate 24. Jasper, "Industries of Jasper" by Alexander Levin (1939).

Plate 25. Houston, "The Houston Ship Canal: Loading Cotton" by Jerry Bywaters (1941).

Plate 26. Kilgore, "Drilling for Oil" (detail) by Xavier Gonzalez (1941).

Plate 27. Liberty, "Story of the Big Fish" by Howard Fisher (1939).

Plate 28. Linden, "Cotton Pickers" (detail) by Victor Arnautoff (1939).

Plate 29. Mart, "McLennan Looking for a Home" by José Aceves (1939).

Plate 30. Ranger, "The Crossroads Town" by Emil Bisttram (1939).

Plate 31. Odessa, "Stampede" (detail) by Tom Lea (1940).

Plate 32. San Antonio, "Agricultural Pursuits" by Howard Cook (1939).

Plate 33. San Antonio, "Trade in San Antonio Plaza" by Howard Cook (1939).

Plate 34. San Antonio, "Houston Presents Sword at First Congress of Texas Republic" by Howard Cook (1939).

Plate 35. San Antonio, "Cattle Trail" by Howard Cook (1939).

Plate 36. Rockdale, "Industry in Rockdale" by Maxwell Starr (1947).

A DIRECTORY OF
TEXAS POST OFFICE MURALS

Alice

"South Texas Panorama"

John Warren Hunter

Unavailable for viewing

4′ × 10′[1]

Oil on canvas

1939

$670

Damaged, in storage at the Smithsonian American
Art Museum

John Warren Hunter's montage of work and industry creates an integrated picture of economic life in early Jim Wells County. The mural reinforces the federal government's message to Americans that hard work and interdependence pointed the way out of the Great Depression. The mural also plays up the prominent role of the U.S. mail in rural communities. A well-dressed rancher, who dominates the right of the mural, stands reading the *Alice Echo* newspaper that evidently has just come in the rural mailbox beside him. Nearby, a cowboy pauses from reading his own letter and gazes reflectively into the distance. By contrast, a second cowboy, on horseback, looks on forlornly, having received no mail.

When Hunter installed his mural, an actual *Alice Echo* article interpreted the painting's message this way: "The old gentleman scans his favorite newspaper for happenings of his county and the doings of the people whose lives are closely bound with his own. Made stern through fluctuating markets and range conditions he [the rancher] nevertheless retains a fine sense of humor and the kindliness that has ever characterized the cowman of the Texas brush country."[2]

The secondary activities in the mural represent other local industries besides ranching. To characterize the oil industry, the artist grouped some workers intently welding and laying oil pipeline. Near an oil derrick and storage tanks, a train of tanker cars invokes the railroad transportation industry. In the center, Mexican workers toil in the field to harvest cotton, and a woman pictured beside a collection wagon weighs her sack of pickings. The artist added a poignant note beside her by including a young child who beckons for attention.

Hunter originally hung the mural in the post office at 71 North Wright Street. Tell-tale areas of paint loss indicate where the canvas was folded when the mural was placed in storage.[3] In 1968, the mural was transferred to the Smithsonian American Art Museum, Washington, D.C., where it remains in storage.

Alpine

"View of Alpine"

José Moya del Pino

Post Office

109 West E Street

4′ × 12′

Oil with tempera underpaint on Masonite

1940

$700

Good condition

Alpine's post office mural reinforced the community's strong sense of identity and the belief that Alpine was the perfect place to live. The mural combines the advantages of both rural and urban life present in this beautiful West Texas mountain community. To express these ideals in his design, the artist set three figures high on a hillside against the backdrop of Alpine's familiar Twin Sisters peaks that overlook Sul Ross State College (now Sul Ross State University) and the city's business district. In the idyllic portrait, all three characters recline comfortably on a ridge and are engrossed in reading. A female student reads from a magazine, while a male student nearby leans on a rock as

he reads a book. A cowboy completes the trio; he concentrates on the tabloid he is holding before him as he leans back, tending his cattle effortlessly while his horse stands nearby. The mural shows the importance of the mail to the cowboy — who is catching up on the latest news in animal husbandry — as well as the importance of Sul Ross State College to Alpine. By extension, the artwork acknowledges the role of the U.S. mail in bringing essential reading material to this remote region. Del Pino portrayed the mail service as a catalyst for bringing news and ideas to help create a balanced society.[4]

If this mural seems a bit self-serving on the part of the federal government, the Section did encourage del Pino to pursue subjects that would be relevant to Alpine residents. As one possibility, Rowan suggested the Spanish explorer Cabeza de Vaca who was said to have reached West Texas. Rowan also portraying prehistoric life, noting that pictographs abound in the region.[5] Del Pino had attempted these subjects in his preliminary sketches; however, he rejected them in favor of highlighting the state college, which local people proudly informed him was more important to the identity of the community.[6]

Alvin

"Emigrants at Nightfall"
Loren Mozley
[Dimensions unknown]
Oil on canvas
1942
$670
Damaged, flaking, in storage

Alvin's post office mural features a pioneer theme, a subject that occurs in several other Texas post office murals as well (for example, Kilgore, Mart). "Emigrants at Nightfall" portrays a small group of early settlers making its way across the prairie in search of a new home. The mural incorporates key frontier values — courage, adventurousness, and determination — all qualities that Roosevelt's New Deal programs were intended to foster. Preparing to camp for the night, the group has paused beside the wagon that contains all the basic necessities to start a new life. In the waning daylight, one member of the group sits on a rock and holds a map outstretched on his knees as he traces the route the group will follow on the next day's journey. Meanwhile, the group's patriarch returns from the hunt, ducks dangling from one hand and his gun on his shoulder. Nearby, his wife focuses all her attention on the infant bundled on her lap. An African American figure is shown carrying firewood. Standing apart, a guide wearing buckskin and a raccoon cap bears a wary expression as he leans on his musket and looks out of the picture as if anticipating the challenges of the westward trek that he knows so well.

The mural had been missing for more than thirty years when, in the 1980s, the postmaster found it folded in storage. During post office renovation, the mural had been peeled away. The City of Alvin eventually purchased the old post office for use as a museum to be maintained by the Alvin Museum Society. The U.S. Postal Service loaned the mural to the group, which plans to have the artwork restored and reinstalled in its post office museum.[7]

Loren Mozley was teaching at the University of Texas art department when he painted his mural for the Alvin post office. Mozley reported that he enjoyed creating the mural and was pleased with how well it fit into the architecture of the lobby.[8] Edward Rowan, chief administrator of the Section of Fine Arts, concurred, calling the work "quite handsome from the standpoint of scale and composition on the wall."[9]

Amarillo

"Coronado's Exploration Party in Palo Duro Canyon,"
"Loading Cattle," "Cattle Branding," "Gang Plow,"
"Disk Harrow," and "Oil" (six panels on four walls)

Julius Woeltz

Federal Courthouse and Post Office

205 East Fifth Street

"Coronado's Exploration Party in Palo Duro Canyon" —
6'6" × 30'1"; "Loading Cattle" — 6'6" × 17'7½"; "Cattle
Branding" — 6'6½" × 6'6½"; "Gang Plow" — 5'10" × 6'6½";
"Disk Harrow" — 5'10" × 6'6½"; and "Oil" — 6'6 12" × 18'¾"

Oil on canvas

1941

$6,500

Excellent condition

History and progress, two recurrent themes in post office murals, combine in Julius Woeltz's Amarillo mural sequence to create a panorama of the Texas Panhandle. Mounted high on the walls of the foyer in the federal courthouse and post office downtown, the six panels trace the high points of the region's historical and industrial development. The murals portray an unbroken chain of progress resulting from high ideals, hard work, and human ingenuity.

The largest of the murals is a montage that stretches thirty-six feet along the entire length of one wall. The painting spans a period from the sixteenth century, when Coronado appeared in nearby Palo Duro Canyon on his quest to find the legendary Seven Cities of Gold, to the early days of cattle drives. The artist compressed time and distance, beginning, at one end of the canvas, with Coronado and his party, who gaze expectantly into the unknown territory, and, symbolically, into the future. In the background, just beyond the adventurers' vision, the spectacle of an Indian buffalo hunt provides the transition to the next scene in the canvas. There, a group of mounted Texas Rangers wielding revolvers encounters a band of shirtless Indians ensconced behind a rock outcropping. Woeltz's cubistic style is evident in shapes of the canyon in

the background and the rendering of brush scattered on the range.

Although Section of Fine Arts policy discouraged violent and unsavory subjects in its post office murals, it overlooked the picturesque portrayal of violence in this mural. One reason for this may have been the artist's abstract, decorative treatment. The Indians, in full headdress and with neatly chiseled torsos, are poised statuesquely aiming their rifles and fully drawn bows at the rangers. Together, these qualities give the mural the quality of a diorama, which seems to create distance from the pictured brutality. Indeed, the Indian lying at the feet of others in his party seems asleep, rather than slain from the fray.

In "Gang Plow" and "Disk Harrow," Woeltz's cubistic style and the perspective created by the vertically arranged furrows create a compelling image that draws the viewer's attention. The converging lines emphasize the apex and the main focus of the painting—a lone farmer sitting atop his new tractor. The image conveys the power of machinery that allows a farmer to transform the face of the land single-handedly, thus creating a statement of faith in modern mechanized agriculture. The image further implies that the new methods will bring an abundance of food. These powerful images must have evoked thoughts of progress and hope in viewers recovering from the Dust Bowl of the previous decade.

The remaining three panels in Woeltz's series depict progress in the chronological development of two other defining Panhandle industries—ranching and oil. Two ranching murals portray typical activities in a West Texas cattle economy. In one, a group of cowboys brands cattle; in the other, livestock board railroad cars for transport to market. A relatively recent addition to Amarillo's history was the oil industry, which Woeltz set against the Panhandle's glowing evening sky. In this final panel, a group of oil workers busily tends the equipment of a modern drilling rig.

Woeltz's murals drew national attention—ironically, much to the artist's distress. A *Time* magazine article stressed the unflattering reactions of a few spectators who quibbled about the murals' details. The magazine reporter, who was present at the dedication of the murals, related with relish how one bystander criticized Woeltz for neglecting to show a shipping pen in one of the ranching murals. Everyone knows, the spectator asserted, that cattle are never loaded on cars directly from the range. Furthermore, the cattle themselves were not authentic, according to another spectator who remarked suspiciously: "Them cattle is mighty clean!" The artist replied defensively, "It has just come a rain." Another spectator accused the artist of painting an English saddle on one of the cowboy's horses, "You couldn't git a cowboy on one of those postage stamp things."[10] The artist bristled especially at this last remark, for he had grown up on a ranch, and he took particular umbrage at the implication that he did not know his saddles. To set the record straight and to discredit the article, Woeltz immediately penned a letter to the editor of *Time* and expressed his annoyance at the article's unfair, narrow treatment that ridiculed his work nationally. Concerning the remark about saddles, he asserted, "Being no stranger in the West, it is inconceivable for me to have placed an English saddle in a western setting. On many occasions, a western saddle had made an impression upon me that can only be called indelible."[11]

The Section of Fine Arts competition for the Amarillo post office murals was one of 190 held regionally across the country.[12] The Section awarded smaller mural commissions in Texas and elsewhere to artists who placed well in the regional and national competitions. Of the sixty-four artists competing for the Amarillo job, many were from Texas; others hailed from Arkansas, Colorado, Kansas, Louisiana, Missouri, New Mexico, and Oklahoma.[13]

Anson

"Cowboy Dance"

Jenne Magafan

Post Office

1002 Eleventh Street

6′11″ × 11′10″

Oil on canvas

1941

$900

Good condition

Jenne Magafan visited Anson to seek an appropriate subject for her post office mural. To her delight, she discovered that on an evening each year in mid-December folks dressed up in cowboy outfits to square dance the way their grandparents had done.

Anson residents seemed to like the artist's preliminary sketch, and Section leaders told Magafan to continue with the full-scale mural. As an afterthought, she added a little brown jug to the lower right corner of the canvas. This seemingly charming embellishment effectively alienated a good many Ansonites and drew a volley of criticisms that proved embarrassing for the artist and for the Section, because Anson was a "dry" town. "Evidently," one citizen pointed out in a letter to the local newspaper, "Miss Magafan did not realize that throughout the history of Anson there has never been an open saloon, nor did she know that the people of Anson continue to vote against liquor stores. Had the artist realized this perhaps she would have omitted the obnoxious liquor jug."[14] The artist's oversight, another citizen commented, signified a careless disregard of the community and was an insult to its upright moral character. One resident complained about the esthetic qualities of the mural, expressing outrage at the offensive "carnival curtain." For others, however, the mural was delightful: "a wonderful work of art, and I am sending people from Stamford [Texas] to see it." Another citizen called the mural lovely and colorful, a "good work of modern art."[15]

Arlington

"Gathering Pecans"
Otis Dozier
Arlington ISD Tax Office, former post office
200 West Main Street
4′ × 12′
Oil on canvas
1941
$750
Good condition

Otis Dozier admitted after being awarded the commission for the Arlington mural, "Since Arlington is a town with no one large industry and little color to its history, it has been difficult to decide on subject matter." He sent Rowan three preliminary sketches of scenes from the cotton, pecan, and dairy industries.[16] Section administrators found the composition of the pecan-gathering scene interesting and unusual.

Dozier's mural shows several family members industriously harvesting pecans from the ground. It subtly places the federal government in a favorable light and extols the practical benefits of scientific research. The artist had learned that, during the 1930s, North Texas Agricultural College offered a federally supported program in pecan propagation and orchard planning.[17] The college strongly encouraged commercial interest in pecans by offering courses sponsored by the U.S. Department of Agriculture. Dozier saw this as an opportunity to recognize the federal government for its efforts to assist the rural economy. The new industry's economic benefit seems to be symbolized by a new, red pickup truck in the background of the mural.

The Arlington postmaster reported the public's reaction to the mural: "Mr. Dozier has just installed the Mural, and we are delighted with it, it is very pretty and is suitable for this Locality. This Mural exceeded our expectation, of course we had no Idea what it would look like, and every one that has seen it compliments it highly."[18]

Baytown

"Texas"
Barse Miller
Baytown Historical Museum (former post office)
220 West Defee Street
5'5" × 10'
Fresco secco (tempera, egg, and oil on dry plaster)
1938
$610
Poor condition, faded, flaking, nearly invisible

The Baytown mural, which focuses on the development of transportation, takes the form of a fantastic allegory.[19] A shirtless, winged giant wearing a raccoon-skin cap dominates the mural. The towering figure — the personification of Texas Progress — with his head in the clouds holds a toy-like airplane in one hand as if to launch it. At the base of the mural, early forms of transportation used to deliver the U.S. mail, including a mule-drawn covered wagon and an early steam locomotive, parade before the giant. In the upper right of the mural, a stars-and-stripes emblem suggests a postage cancellation mark.

Good public relations took precedence over artistic freedom in the making of this mural. Section of Fine Arts administrators, ever cautious not to offend the public, encouraged the artist to lessen the amount of skin exposed in the original mural design. Edward Rowan assured Miller that the Section was not trying to coerce the artist into painting in a way not consistent with his convictions. Nevertheless, he did need to cover at least the figure's lower body: "You have placed unusual emphasis on the torso of the figure, and we frankly feel that a good many people would be justified in objecting to the insistent nudity of the figure."[20] The artist readily complied by raising the position of the hero's loin cloth and making the transportation vehicles parading across the painting larger to distract attention from the giant's nudity.

The City of Baytown purchased the post office building in 1985 when the postal service moved to a new facility. The old building then became the Baytown Historical Museum.

Big Spring

"O Pioneers"

Peter Hurd

Howard County Public Library (former post office)

312 Scurry Street

6′ × 26′

Fresco

1938

$1,300

Some cracking

This mural's domestic scene on the West Texas prairie presents a nostalgic view of pioneer family life. Poised before a sod house at sunset, a family of settlers prepares to end its work day. The father with one arm akimbo stands with his musket stock planted on the ground. His wife stands behind him and holds their child in her arms. Two older children complete the final chores before nightfall. The young daughter goes to fetch water in her bucket, and the boy prods two oxen yoked to a simple plow. Several chickens busily peck the ground nearby as horses graze in the field. A wagon protrudes from behind the cabin, suggesting the means of the family's arrival on the plains. In the distance, pink clouds outline a mesa.

The Section of Fine Arts staff cultivated the image of stability of frontier subjects. Thus, Rowan suggested that Peter Hurd add certain details to the mural, including the chickens and clothes hanging on the line to dry, to suggest "elements of a slightly personal nature," which indicated a permanent settlement. The inclusion of fat chickens in a rough frontier setting also reinforced the formula that the federal officials wanted to encourage, that is, that hard work leads inevitably to prosperity.

Hurd was careful to incorporate local scenery in his mural, including Signal Mountain, one of Big Spring's identifying features. The mesa, which rises 2,700 feet above the plain about ten miles southeast of Big Spring, derives its name from the Indian practice of sending smoke signals up from its flat top. Local legend held that a cache of gold sat at the bottom of one of the mountain's deep fissures.

In a time when traditional male breadwinners found themselves unemployed, sometimes straining family solidarity, Hurd's mural verifies historically that family and frontier values will bring prosperity. The pioneer family, advancing despite hardships, driven by a dream of some future happiness, seemed at the core of democracy, as Hurd's inscription at the bottom of the mural to indicates. Modified from a line by Walt Whitman, the inscription reads: "O pioneers, democracy rests finally upon us, and our visions sweep through eternity."

O PIONEERS. DEMOCRACY RESTS FINALLY UPON US. AND OUR VISIONS SWEEP THROUGH ETERNITY

Hurd noted after completing the mural that people seemed to understand the inscription and the mural itself. "The comments of the people," he observed, "showed they were emotionally aware, through the painting, of the fortitude and determination of these early settlers and of the character and mettle it took to be among those first to settle West Texas. And that those qualities must not die in the face of today's problems."[21]

An article in the local newspaper expressed pride in and a sense of elation with the effect of Hurd's work: "Appears this city is destined for the upper strata of culture or something."[22] Many people stood and looked long at the mural each day. "There is [sic] very few days pass," Postmaster Nat Schick wrote, "but, that someone comes to my office to tell me how perfectly beautiful they think it [the mural] is and how much it adds to the appearance of the lobby, and also that it is so much different from any they have ever seen. I know that the patrons of this office are 100% in their praise and appreciation to the Department for having it done."[23]

After Hurd completed the mural, Rowan's final disposition was that the work displayed "competent draftsmanship that is not dried out by the competency."[24] Supreme Court Justice Harlan S. Stone, upon viewing Hurd's mural, made the connection between pioneer values and the present. He commented enthusiastically: "What a lovely composition the Hurd mural is. Aside from all the other considerations, how important it is that the humble people of the country should be impressed with the fact that the artist finds beauty and dignity in their life, and one of the many things that we need to be taught in this country is that our lives, however simple or humble, may be both beautiful and dignified."[25]

Hurd further noted the effect of the mural on a public unaccustomed to art: "The great surprise about this thing," he reported to Rowan, "is the terrific enthusiasm of the public: They are really crazy about it and while not one single person of them has any cultural knowledge of which he could gauge it — and no one has knowledge of the great traditions of painting — yet everyone (hundreds) come in every day stand below my scaffold which is nine feet above the floor and talk."[26]

Painting the Big Spring post office mural was a remarkable experience for Hurd. He was, as many mural artists were, unaccustomed to working in public. Hurd expressed his faith in the potential of the Section of Fine Arts and specifically in its means of bringing about a renaissance in painting in America. Indeed, this was one of the section's goals.[27] Hurd explained to Rowan: "The experience of painting in the public lobby of a post office was one of the most exciting I have ever had: The crowds that gathered below the scaffold — mostly plainsmen, ranchers and farmers, with their constant and audible comment was a new experience. At times this continual chatter was harassing when I was at something which required particular and especial concentration. But it wasn't long until I learned how to tune out their voices at these times."[28] But the chatter the artist perceived below were echoes of people awakening to art. "When at first the scaffold was set up," Hurd related, "and the old plaster removed there was practically no interest at all on the part of the public who came in and out of the post office. But as soon as the fresco began to develop there was such an enthusiastic and generally favorable . . . reaction on the part of the many who saw it that I was amazed. I certainly had not expected any such response and wouldn't have been in the least surprised at a general apathy with perhaps a few of the people interested and understanding."[29]

Today, the former Big Spring post office is the Howard County Public Library. Hurd's handsome fresco daily greets patrons of all ages as they pass beneath it on their way to the book check-out counter.

Borger

"Big City News"

José Aceves

Hutchinson County Historical Museum

618 North Main Street

4′5″ × 9′7¼″

Oil on canvas

1939

$570

Restored in 1981

Early ranching days provided the setting of the mural created for the Borger post office. José Aceves pictured Borger's first wooden buildings, including the barber shop and, of course, the post office. In this variation of a common theme involving the mail, two cowboys are shown standing on the boardwalk outside the post office. They are "hungry for the big city news," as the artist unequivo-cally stated.[30] One cowboy eagerly reads a letter he has just received as a second cowhand peers over his shoulder. In the background, a third cowboy clutching a piece of paper strides urgently toward the post office entrance. Two horses prominently tied to the post nearby complete the picture's western flavor.

In the late 1970s, the mural was removed from the old post office when the postal service abandoned that building. Local residents successfully petitioned the federal government to restore the artwork, and it subsequently was given to the community on long-term loan.[31] Ed Benz, of Borger, recalled fondly: "When I was a youth the mural was . . . an extra-special part of going to the post office with my dad. I think everybody noticed it; it was part of their lives."[32] Later in his life, as director of the Hutchinson County Museum, Benz was able to view the mural every day in the museum where it is displayed today.

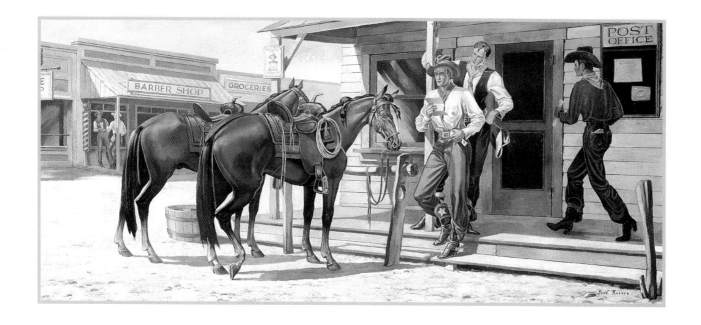

Brady

"Texas Immigrants"

Gordon K. Grant

Post Office

2295 Blackburn Street

4′ × 10′

Oil on canvas

1939

$620

Good condition

"The Texas Immigrants" portrays a dramatic moment when, in their journey westward, a family of settlers turns to view a startling spectacle in the distance. From their vantage point on a ridge overlooking the vast prairie, members of the group are transfixed by the sight of a band of Indian hunters pursuing a herd of buffalo. The boy and his mother view the scene curiously from their position seated on the covered wagon, while a member of the group on horseback, riding with longhorn cattle, points excitedly and with apprehension to the spectacle. In the foreground, the father is mounted on horseback; the prominence of the rifle he carries adds tension to the mural story,

as it suggests the potential danger and his readiness to defend his family against attack. The whole scene glows with the reddish brown light typical of a western prairie.

The artist, Gordon Grant, who lived in Santa Barbara, California, could not easily travel to Brady, Texas, to research subjects and the Texas landscape for his murals. The Section allowed artists no extra funds for travel expenses; when artists received a mural commission far from home, travel expenses sometimes cut deeply into their budget. Grant relied instead on library research at home, written communication with the postmaster, and his own imagination to complete the mural with authenticity—all with considerable success. When Brady citizens saw the completed mural, they seemed to marvel at Grant's talent, as a local newspaper headline suggests: "ARTIST WHO PAINTED 'LONGHORNS' ON POST OFFICE MURAL HAS NEVER SEEN A LONGHORN."[33] The artist observed that "everyone who came into the lobby at the time of its mounting . . . expressed their delight in having a hand painted picture of early Texas immigrants."[34] Brady's postmaster, who had immigrated to Texas in 1873, was pleased with Grant's mural, and people came from miles around to see it installed in April, 1939.[35]

Brownfield

"Ranchers of the Panhandle Fighting Prairie Fire with Skinned Steer"

Frank Mechau

Brownfield Police Department (former post office)

120 North Fifth Street

5′6″ × 12′

Oil on canvas

1940

$750

Excellent condition, restored in the 1980s through citizen fund-raising efforts

Few Section of Fine Arts murals in Texas involved as much disagreement over subject matter as did Brownfield's mural, which some viewers considered gruesome. Frank Mechau wanted to depict a graphic but practical — and, by his claim, authentic — method ranchers used at one time to control prairie fires. He decided on the unusual subject after talking with retired ranchers and old cowboys. Mechau's research revealed that cowboys would create a fire line by killing a steer, skinning it, and then dragging the carcass along the edge of the fire to halt the progress of the blaze. James Dallas, the Brownfield postmaster, voiced his apprehension upon learning that a mural was to be installed in his post office. "I am wondering if we will be given a chance to say what we would like to have on this mural," Dallas wrote to S. W. Purdum, fourth assistant postmaster general. "I will be frank with you," he added, "that there are some murals that I don't care about having around the office. I would appreciate it very much if you could allow us a little 'say so' in this matter."[36] Evidently he had heard of post office mural subject controversies in other parts of the country.[37]

When Rowan read the postmaster's letter, he realized that the artist had failed to consult with the postmaster re-

garding the mural's subject. He shared the postmaster's concerns with the artist and expressed disappointment at the way Mechau had handled the matter, suggesting that the artist write an explanation to Dallas.[38] Mechau, who was well underway with his painting, cringed. In his reply to Rowan, he characterized the postmaster's comments as "prematurely belligerent," adding, "I hope we won't have trouble with this gentleman who does not seem to like the idea of murals in his office very well."[39]

Rowan then sent Dallas a photograph of the artist's work in progress. Dallas predictably objected in his response to Rowan but added a new twist. "Frankly, I am disappointed in it," he wrote. "I like the idea fine because a scene such as this depicts was a very common occurance [sic] in this section up until a few years ago [that is, prairie fires], but the cowboys [in Mechau's painting] do not look like our kind. They look to [sic] much like Spaniards. Another thing, as best as I can learn out here they never did skin a beef to put out fires. They usually killed the beef but they never did take the time to skin one in a hurry. They could not take the time. They drug [sic] them like they were. They had to do something in a hurry. Another thing[:] we never had any stirrups like he [Mechau] has shown on the saddles."[40]

Dallas revealed that he had wanted "something more realistic," specifically, a scene from the historic ranch of the town's founder, M. V. Brownfield, which he believed local residents would like better. He stressed that resident ranchers would pinpoint inaccuracies in Mechau's current mural. Finally, Dallas — considering that he may not be able to have his way — asked that Mechau at least change the mural's title to "Ranchers of West Texas Dragging a Prairie Fire with a Steer."[41]

Mechau meanwhile wrote a somewhat conciliatory letter to Dallas, assuring him of the authenticity of his treatment. He cited his interviews with several reliable old ranchers of the Southwest, including Frank Gilpin, one of the "old boys who knew all the trails from Mexico to Canada." Mechau detailed the grisly procedure, according to Gilpin. "Steers," wrote Mechau, "were skinned down to the rump, the wet skin dragging behind the carcass to serve as a wet blanket. The head was either roped up to the legs or sometimes cut off as the horns occasionally caught in the ground making rough going for the ponies. If there was sufficient time or help available, they sometimes gutted the steer to lighten the weight. The heat was often so intense and the ground so hot that the cow ponies had to be constantly changed from inside the flame to outside to save their hooves which were sometimes so badly burned they fell off."[42] Mechau also claimed to have consulted an authoritative book on Charles Goodnight — the famous Chisholm Trail cattle driver from Texas — which had led him to the same conclusion that the steers were skinned.

Mechau answered the postmaster's other criticisms: "You will find that cowboys and ranchers of the time depicted often used tapaderos on their stirrups even though they might not be functional in western Texas they were dressy and God knows the boys seemed to like that sort of thing. I used them in my mural because they added to the forward speed and movement of the picture." Finally, addressing the postmaster's remark about the ethnic appearance of the figures in the mural, Mechau wrote sardonically: "They might well look greasy after fighting fire and smoke for a few days. However, I shall see to it that they have a Nordic profile and a blue eye shining through the sweat."[43]

Mechau had progressed too far on the mural to start over. As a solution, Rowan persuaded the artist to compromise by keeping the steer's head in the mural but making the steer's skinned condition less prominent. Rowan further appeased Dallas by seeking additional funds for the painting of a second mural to depict the Brownfield ranch.[44]

When the artist personally visited Brownfield on his way to begin work on his murals for the downtown Fort Worth courthouse and post office, the strained relationship that had developed between Dallas and Mechau suddenly seemed to dissolve. Mechau met Dallas and some other residents and charmed them all. By the time he left Brownfield for Fort Worth, Mechau had managed to transform the built-up hostilities with Dallas into good will. Thenceforth, the whole tone of Dallas's correspondence, starting with the salutations, took on a tone of familiarity. He addressed the artist amicably as, "The Honorable Frank Mechau" and "Dear Frank." When Dallas saw a photograph of the completed, modified mural, he quipped to Mechau: "Boy, do I like that mural a lot better." He added in jest: "If you keep on you will get good one of these days. No foolin' I like it."[45]

Mechau's charm during his visit prompted several young men, including the postmaster, to plan a surprise for the artist when he returned to install the mural. Dallas confided to Rowan, "To get in the proper mind for a western mural, and also as a take off on old Frank [Mechau wore a beard] we have all grown a beard for at least six weeks." Meanwhile, the mural had been shipped to the post office to await the artist's arrival. However, weeks went by, and still Mechau did not show up. Dallas wrote to Rowan: "Some of the boys have taken out but there are still three of us left. It looks like we are going to be forced to shave. We got such a kick out of Mechau and his whiskers that we thought he would really get a kick out of ours."[46] Dallas finally received the disappointing news about bureaucratic delays on federal permission to install the mural. The artist had to leave for his fall teaching obligations at Columbia University and could not install the mural himself. He arranged for an "able assistant" from Dallas to travel to Brownfield when approval came from Washington.

The episode ended anticlimactically with the installation in October. A newspaper account reported simply: "After many weeks of waiting the mural was hung without ceremony."[47] Two months later, Rowan queried the postmaster about the installation. Dallas returned Rowan's note with these words scribbled on it: "Everything is fine. Mural is up. Everybody happy. Lots of criticism — lots of praise. Wish I had time to write you more."[48] The Section of Fine Arts ceased operation before Brownfield's second mural could be arranged.

Bryan

"Bison Hunt"

William Gordon Huff

Bryan Federal Building (former post office)

Twenty-sixth and Parker Streets

4'9" × 7'6"

Terrazzo relief (lunette)

1941

$1,000

Good condition

William Huff's relief sculpture of an Indian buffalo hunt for the Bryan post office is made of terrazzo (a cast stone composed of crushed marble, pigment, and cement). The lunette shows two stampeding buffaloes. Wounded by Indian arrows, the buffaloes are shown collapsing as their front legs buckle under their massive weight. The federal press release announcing the installation of the panel describes the composition nostalgically: "Though held within the framework of a semi-circle, the sculpture gives us a feeling of unrestricted physical movement which the Bison once knew on the mesa of Texas."[49]

Mural artists were encouraged to choose subjects that reflected local interest and activity for a mural subject. Huff's choice of buffalo was a stretch. He skipped over the cattle and ranching industries as possible subjects because they were no longer of any consequence in Bryan. He also rejected cotton as a subject, despite its being a major local industry. Instead, he chose bison because he was impressed with stories of herds of bison that once roamed in Texas.[50] Although there were no bison herds in the immediate vicinity of Bryan, Huff rationalized his choice to the section by saying that buffalo herds were in the Austin area, only one hundred miles from Bryan.[51]

The public reacted favorably to the mural. One fastidious observer, however, demanded more authenticity. The post office janitor complained about the buffaloes' color. He also wanted to know why the sky was not painted blue and "why the gleam in the buffaloes' eyes was not painted in." Annoyed with such minutiae, Huff speculated sarcastically, "If I had done all that and in addition glued real hair to the modeled animals he [the janitor] would have been pleased — or imagined that he would."[52]

Caldwell

"Indians Moving"

Suzanne Scheuer
Burleson County Courthouse
205 West Buck Street
5′ × 12′6″
Oil on canvas
1939
$710
Restored in 1989, moved to courthouse after demolition
of old post office

Suzanne Scheuer captured the slow and deliberate migration of a group of nomadic Plains Indians in this mural. Several female Indians parade together on horseback; their travois loaded with their belongings drag behind them. Children of different ages trail along on foot and ride with their mothers. In the background, two male Indians on horseback complete the grouping.

On the surface, "Indians Moving" is a romantic picture of the cyclic migration of Plains Indians. It is also a subtle criticism on the federal government's policy that displaced the Indians. As Scheuer's words confirm, the mural indirectly expresses the artist's sympathies with the unfair treatment of Indians who were ousted from their homes and forced to march across the country to Indian Territory in Oklahoma during the nineteenth century. In a local newspaper interview, Scheuer stated that the mural suggests the "American Indian moving 'out of the picture' forever."[53] She did not hesitate to express her views candidly: "I am interested in the American Indian and feel sympathetic towards that race of people which was so speedily eradicated by our present civilization. I believe that a reminder, even though it be in the form of a picture, to any one of us of the life in this country that preceded ours can do no harm, especially since that life, in its simplicity and harmony with nature, can be a lesson to us in many ways."[54]

After Caldwell's old post office was abandoned and destroyed, postal authorities displayed the removed mural for several years in the post office in nearby College Station. (Ironically, the mural by Victor Arnautoff at the College Station post office had already disappeared during the post office renovation in 1962. It is presumed to be destroyed.)[55] After its restoration, the Caldwell mural was installed permanently in the Burleson County Courthouse.

Canyon

"Strays"

Francis S. Ankrom

Post Office

1304 Fourth Avenue

4' × 13'

Oil on canvas

1938

$580

Good condition

Francis Ankrom's mural portrays a group of white-faced Hereford cattle that are stranded in a blind canyon, a common occurrence with free-ranging livestock, in the vicinity of Palo Duro Canyon. The subject is an alternative to Ankrom's preliminary sketches, which the Section of Fine Arts rejected. The story of how "Strays" became the final mural subject illustrates the Section's sensitivity to potentially negative public reaction to certain mural subjects.

Ankrom originally submitted three mural ideas of Indians' being routed. The Section flatly rejected these as unsuitable. One of the rejected sketches, "Rout in Palo Duro," depicted the U.S. Army's bloody, surprise attack in 1874 on a village occupied mostly by Comanche and Kiowa women and children. The attack, which was led by General Ranald Mackenzie, is considered by historians to mark the end of the Indian wars in Texas. Ankrom based his other rejected sketches, "In Defense of the Mail" and "Onward Texas," on Indian warfare. Section officials informed the artist that it was not in the federal government's best interests to exhibit such violent portrayals in public murals. They finally accepted the artist's idea of portraying strays in Palo Duro Canyon — a more politically correct subject.

The mural was removed from the old post office in January, 1979, restored, and reinstalled in 1982.[56]

Center

"Logging Scene"

Edward Chavez

Post Office

101 Tenaha Street

4′ × 11′11″

Oil on canvas

1941

$670

Good condition

Edward Chavez chose a subject suitable for Center, a community located in the heart of East Texas' Piney Woods region. At the time of the mural, hauling logs by ox-wagon was being replaced by modern trucks, and in his mural Chavez wanted to invoke the historically important values associated with manual labor. According to the artist, part of the richness associated with earlier methods — that is, the human exchange among workers — was less likely to be encouraged in an industry that had become mechanized.

The mural portrays a quaint view of early logging in an East Texas. Against a background of a pine forest that has been clear-cut, the mural depicts a group of loggers beside a halted, oxen-drawn wagon bearing two huge logs. The lumbermen are painted socializing with fellow workers who sit to rest on top of their cargo. A vulture glides above a few scrawny pine trees left standing against gray sky. Two of the mural's side panels depict the manual tools used in logging.

The Section of Fine Arts approved Chavez's original sketch with reservations. Rowan criticized the rhythm of the design and suggested ways to make the composition and the figures appear more authentic. Rowan's comment to Chavez indicates the esthetic preferences for realism of members of the section. However, the Section was also attempting to help Chavez improve his technical skills. "It is our [the Section administrators'] feeling," Rowan wrote to the artist, "that more personal observation on your part must be reflected in the execution of this work in order to give every element the stamp of authenticity which is a characteristic of all good painting regardless of the approach."[57] The artist worked out the technical problems, and the Section approved the mural.

Clifton

"Texas Longhorns—A Vanishing Breed"

Ila McAfee

Post Office

407 West Fifth Street

4′9″ × 11′8″

Oil on canvas

1941

$700

Canvas torn due to crack in wall

In this lofty depiction of the Texas longhorn, Ila McAfee portrays a white specimen of the legendary breed standing majestically high on a pedestal-like rock in the center of the picture. The regal animal overlooks the other members of the grazing herd on the rolling plains. Two bulls in the foreground lock horns as other steers nearby retain their serene indifference amid the prickly pear cactus.

McAfee was fascinated by the longhorn's importance in Texas history. She also declared that the longhorn was "still very dear to the old timers."[58] Longhorns, once prevalent in the nineteenth- and early-twentieth-century cattle drives through the area around Clifton, were by the 1930s all but extinct. McAfee was enthusiastic about longhorns as a mural subject, but she had to overcome local resistance to get her way. For Clifton residents, longhorns did not seem as glamorous or intriguing as another subject that the postmaster insisted McAfee paint: an old mill. A mural featuring the mill, which dated to the Civil War era but was no longer in operational, would please the postmaster as well as others of the community more than anything else. The crumbled ruin of the mill was located on the site of old Clifton, but romantic images of it intact showed up in places all about town, including prints that hung in people's homes and even a painting of the icon on the curtain of the local theater.

Despite its dearness to residents' hearts, McAfee was against focusing her mural on the mill. "I just can't see it as a mural," McAfee complained to Rowan, "and anyway I want to do Longhorns."[59] She then offered authoritative evidence of the longhorn's significance to the region by citing J. Frank Dobie, well-known Texas folklorist.[60] McAfee argued cleverly against the mill as a subject, writing to the postmaster: "The mill would be very difficult for me to reproduce to satisfy the people who know it and its background. . . . It is not very likely it [McAfee's painting] would be convincing to the ones of you who know it [the mill] well."[61]

Rowan explained to the postmaster that Section of Fine Arts administrators favored the artist's idea of longhorns for a mural and that another public image of the mill would be redundant. Stating the case about the cattle, Rowan cited Dobie as an authority on the subject and asserted hyperbolically with obvious relish: "In view of the fact that the Longhorn has made more history than any other breed of animal the civilized world has ever known it is our feeling that the subject is in every way dignified and appropriate."[62]

The longhorn proved ultimately to be a good subject choice, reaping praise from residents. Even the postmaster finally had to agree. After seeing the completed work, he commented earnestly: "Miss McAfee has done a splendid piece of work in this mural, and, from all indications, our people are very well pleased. I judge by the remarks I hear as the people view it while here in our lobby."[63]

An article in the local newspaper gloated: "Volumes could be written about the Texas Longhorn, but in this limited space it can only be said that the Texas Longhorn, rough, rangy, unlovely and wild, able to exist without care, was the reason for, the sole cause of America's Romance of Cattle. . . . this country, and Texas in particular should hold in honored memory — the Texas Longhorn."[64]

College Station

"Good Technique—Good Harvest"

Victor M. Arnautoff

Unavailable for viewing

[Dimensions unknown]

Oil on canvas

1938

$710

Lost, presumed destroyed during building renovation in 1962

Some artists succeeded in getting the Section of Fine Arts to approve the first mural subjects they submitted. Others, such as Victor Arnautoff, almost struck out. The Section vetoed his first two sketches for the College Station mural because of their poor taste. In one design the artist had tied the Greek myth of Icarus and Dedalus to the development of modern flight. This might have been a good idea in itself, but Section officials regarded it as an ironic choice to illustrate the progress of aviation, especially because it is a story of *failed* flight! In the myth, Icarus leaps from a cliff and begins to fly on a pair of artificial wings that his father fashioned out of wax. When Icarus soars too close to the sun, against his father's advice, the wax on the wings melts, and the young daredevil falls from the sky to his death. Arnautoff also made the mistake of including an air disaster in the background of his sketch.[65] Section officials reasoned that Icarus would remind people that high-flying progress could sputter and crash, much like Arnautoff's second mural idea. On the proposed panels, titled "Nothing" and "Plenty," he would portray the use of primitive tools next to the uses of modern machinery.[66] When the Section rejected this sketch, the artist deferred to the general theme of petroleum and agriculture—what College Station leaders had wanted initially to represent vital industries.[67]

One of the prominent vignettes depicted in Arnautoff's busy montage of cotton and oil is the dramatic moment when a field worker brings his sack of cotton to the scale to be weighed. Because cotton pickers were paid by the pound, all eyes in the painting are fixed on the scale operated by the severe-looking foreman. The picture exudes an aura of anticipation mixed with suspicion; perhaps the scales did not always tell the truth. The mural's secondary images include a group of African American female field workers stooped low to pick cotton. With one

knee to the ground, each of them toils to drag a long, white canvas bag of cotton. The mural also presents a microcosm of the depression-era social structure. In the central middle distance, for example, in contrast to the manual laborers, the worker at the scale weighing the basket of cotton that the African American figure brings to it is white. Also, a white man sits comfortably in a tractor and shifts gears to thrust the machine forward. The mural also includes symbols of prosperity, as it shows numerous oil derricks standing farther in the distance; one of the wells has come in and spurts oil into the air before it is capped.

Arnautoff completed his preliminary drawing by September, 1938, sending the required photographs of it to Washington for final approval. Rowan spared no praise for the work. Speaking for the Section judges, he informed the artist unequivocally: "The cartoon gave us the opportunity to see how consummate a work of art you have created for the decoration. The drawing of the four women gathering cotton is as beautiful a passage as we have seen in many a moon and to say that everybody who has seen it is enthusiastic is putting it mildly. My only hope is that the people of College Station will enjoy it as much as we have."[68] What began on shaky ground, ended in triumph.

Conroe

"Early Texans"
Nicholas Lyon
Unavailable for viewing
5'6" × 14'
Oil on canvas
1938
$660
Destroyed

The old post office at Conroe is now a police station. Little public information is known about the disappearance of this mural. As most murals that feature the subject of settlement, "Early Texans" presented values associated with westward migration—people relying on primitive tools, methods, and, perhaps most importantly, on their intrepid will. American individualism and fortitude were favored themes of Roosevelt's New Deal programs, and Lyon's character portrayal served the Section of Fine Arts well. A young couple dominates the central portion of the picture's pioneer party. They are standing together as if transfixed by something in the distance, outside the picture. Their forward-looking gaze suggests their courage at

facing the unknown. The central figure and leader of the party holds his musket upright by the barrel, while his wife embraces what seems to be a religious figure of the Virgin and Child — symbols of human faith and hope. Crouching nearby, a young man holds a musket, while two youngsters — one of them clutching a rooster — stand restlessly behind him. A guide wearing buckskin and a raccoon-skin hat stands to one side by his horse. Unlike the others, he stares *into* the picture at the other characters who are in his care. The setting seems to be a rest stop for settlers, a fact suggested by the appearance of an adobe structure, possibly a supply store, protruding into the picture. Nearby, a man tends his burro as a pair of excited geese seem to honk frantically from their small pen.

As with numerous other post office mural creations, the original conception of Conroe's mural was quite different from the one that finally took a place on the post office wall. Lyon's preliminary sketches featured elements of the oil industry. During a trip to visit the oil fields of Conroe and watch the operations, he talked to a number of experts and "tried to catch something of the mobile massiveness of oil in these sketches."[69] However, for all his efforts, the Section was not satisfied with his design. Although Rowan found the sketch pleasant enough, he reasoned that the people would not appreciate it because the artist's rendition was too abstract and "not sufficiently self-explanatory." Rowan, therefore, requested that Lyon make it more "factual."[70] Lyon redrew the sketches, trying to im-

plement Rowan's suggestions. Still Rowan was not convinced. He asked Lyon to develop a completely new idea using elements from the sketch that the artist had submitted for the San Antonio competition.

Lyon, again, patiently complied. As an objective outside observer, he made some observations about Conroe and its residents that now are historically interesting. This exemplifies how post office murals are not only works of art but artifacts that — together with the comments of artists — offer later generations insight into the culture of the time. The artist agreed to make a second trip to Conroe to deepen his knowledge of the place before beginning his new design. Lyon was able to blend his portrayal of the subject of Conroe's settlement with a good representation of his keen observations of the landscape and the character of the people. He explained to Rowan: "There are pines and palmettos and a sort of comfortable activity caused by an abundance of the necessities of life, yet the people are full of new ideas and interests. They are especially proud of the fact that there is none of the wild spending connected with early 'boom towns' and that they are building slowly and permanently. I have tried with this sketch to depict the youthful spirit and natural abundance of East Texas with things familiar to everyone there."[71] After suggesting several improvements in the design, such as adjusting the size of the hunter's head, which seemed to Rowan to be proportionately too small, the Section finally gave its approval, and Lyon completed the mural.[72]

Cooper

"Before the Fencing of Delta County"

Lloyd Goff

Post Office

150 East Dallas Avenue

4′4″ × 9′

Oil and tempera on canvas

1939

$560

Good condition

Lloyd Goff had an amusing time painting this quasi-caricature of a group of untidy, trail-worn cowboys pausing for a water break. One cowpoke, who is pictured with his shirt off to reveal his sunburned arms and bulging biceps, takes a long swig from a wooden bucket. Goff played up the Texas cowpoke stereotype further by prominently placing a sun-bleached cow's skull, flag-like, on a pole. A cowpuncher on horseback and a longhorn saunter along in the background to complete the arrangement of props for this imaginative Texas vignette.

Despite the playful treatment of the mural's subject matter, authenticity of the figures emerged as one of Goff's central concerns. He had reworked the sketch that he had submitted for the Dallas post office mural competition. In that design, the figures originally did not fit Section administrators' idea of cowboys. They told the artist that the cowboys in the sketch seemed too gentlemanly and needed to be made into typical "cowboy types and not handsome types of Dude-ranchers."[73] Goff, therefore, proceeded to transform the figures as "more rugged types," with satisfactory results.[74]

Participation in the Section of Fine Arts program helped artists advance their careers while affording them the unusual chance to encounter the public directly. After completing the mural at Cooper, Goff acknowledged that the reception and encouragement of local residents made his effort more worthwhile than the remunerative value of the job. "I learned a great deal," he admitted. "The appreciation of the townspeople, farmers, cowhands, and workers was the most encouraging I've ever had. The humble praise of the simple folk was an inspiration. One farmer declared in his most complimentary expression that the mural was, 'Right plain.' Another said it was, 'Plain natural.'"[75]

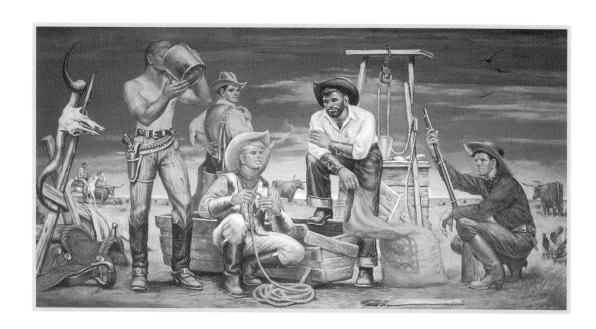

Corpus Christi

**"The Sea: Port Activities and Harbor Fisheries"
and "The Land: Agriculture, Mineral Resources,
and Ranching"**

Howard Cook

Nueces County Courthouse

901 Leopold Street

Two panels — 4′ × 17′ each

Oil on canvas

1941

$3,000

Good condition

The murals were removed from the post office in 1978, rolled up, and stored in the Nueces County Courthouse vault. Several years later, local residents convinced postal officials to agree to install the murals in the new courthouse, where they are located today in opposite corners of the mezzanine level of the courthouse atrium.

After spending several days in Corpus Christi to visit the post office and to sketch typical scenes of local industries, Cook was impressed with the bustling activities of the region. He explained the motives for his choice of subject in this way: "The city is young, growing fast and youthfully proud of its achievements. . . . These are the essential values of the community, . . . so it seemed important to play on the contemporary scene as a subject matter."[76]

One of Cook's two montages depicts sea-related activities of the Gulf Coast city, and the other portrays land-related industries. "The Land" depicts ranching in South Texas: a mounted cowboy — cigarette dangling from his mouth — tends white-face cattle. In addition, Cook portrayed agricultural abundance by showing workers engaged in various activities that he had observed: one woman at an outdoor stand arranges produce; another woman picks citrus fruit. A laborer, head lowered, picks cotton while behind him another worker hefts a crate of produce on his shoulder. Farther in the background, a farmer is at work with his tractor and gang plow, while a pipe spews water into the irrigation ditch. In addition to farming, leisure activities in connection with the land are represented by a hunter crouched behind a bush blind as he spots a deer. He has already bagged a mallard, which indicates the natural abundance of wildlife in the region. "The Sea" portrays fishing along the coast, longshoremen carting cotton, an oil tanker, scenes from the Port of Corpus Christi, and a chemical plant. The images symbolize ways that the modern world — including the city of Corpus Christi — uses natural resources to bring prosperity.

Artists considered decorative components when creating post office murals. Cook, for example, made his murals in a "light blonde key to harmonize with the freshness and crisp airiness of the interior." He chose the color design "to tie in with the clean walls and to repeat notes of white interior venetian blinds, dark lavender shell-color marble bands, gray floor and polished brass and bronze fixtures."[77] The post office Cook described, however, is now destroyed.

Dallas

"Pioneer Homebuilders" (main panel, north wall) and "Airmail" (west wall)

Peter Hurd

Federal office building (formerly, the U.S. Post Office Terminal Annex Building; public access limited)

205 East Houston Street

"Pioneer Homebuilders"—8'4" × 19'8"; "Airmail Over Texas"—8'4" × 4'20"

Fresco

1940

$7,200

Good condition

Recalling the frontier American value of neighbor helping neighbor, the main panel for the Dallas parcel post building, formerly known as the Terminal Annex building, portrays a group of Texas pioneers engaged in a house raising. The central image portrays neighbors pitching in to build a log cabin for a family of newcomers, while, to the right,

where an open fire issues a column of smoke, two women cook beside the wagon that transported the settlers to their new home site. A little girl (a portrait of the artist's daughter) stands with the woman under a canopy, while a teenage girl carries two buckets of water toward the cooking area.[78]

The tall and narrow panel, "Airmail Over Texas," showcases the advancement of night airmail delivery. Beacon lights helped make night flights possible, and Hurd's mural shows a contemporary airplane flying overhead as it passes dramatically through a cone of light coming from a ground beacon. A rural mail box prominently placed in the foreground of the mural stands before a farmhouse to round out the visual anecdote. Hurd consciously tried to depict the landscape between Pecos and El Paso, the route of the Western Airlines airmail flights.[79]

Ironically, perhaps, bitter controversy preceded Hurd's painting of the scene of neighborliness and harmony in "Pioneer Homebuilders." The Section had originally selected two "outsiders," Lucien Labaudt and Edward Biber-

man of San Francisco, to paint the Dallas mural. A group of twelve Dallas artists, led by Jerry Bywaters and Alexandre Hogue, cried foul. The California artists had won honorable mention in the San Antonio competition, but the enraged Dallas artists believed that the Dallas commission should have gone to a local artist.

The Texans claimed that they were not given a fair chance to compete for a local commission.[80] They argued that Dallas was important enough to have its own, separate competition, given that four million people lived within a hundred-mile radius.[81] They contended that outsiders had little knowledge of Texas and would be handicapped in their research by living a great distance from Dallas.[82] Finally, the Texans claimed that the Section had deceived them, citing "at least four letters" from Washington that stated there would be either no mural for Dallas or there would be a competition. Perhaps feeding their passionate response was the artists' lingering resentment at being passed over by the 1936 Texas Centennial Committee to decorate the Hall of State building at Fair Park. That job also was awarded to non-Texas artists.[83]

Congressman Hatton W. Sumners took the Dallas artists' side and criticized the Section directly.[84] In response to a request from the drama editor of the Dallas *Daily Times Herald* for an explanation of the affair, Rowan meticulously challenged the accusation of unfairness, pointing out that Texas artists, including those from Dallas, had had two previous chances to compete in regional competitions that year — in El Paso and Phoenix. They also had the opportunity to compete in two national competitions — one for the San Antonio post office and federal building and one for the Department of the Interior building in Washington. According to Rowan, except for Tom Lea's submission, "the entries of Texas artists did not hold their own, in the opinion of our juries, with the work submitted by the two California artists in these competitions." The juries, he continued, were made up of twenty members from different parts of the country, representing different regions.[85]

To appease the Dallas group, however, and to avoid bad publicity, Rowan boldly recalled the commission from Biberman and Labaudt and organized a separate competition just for Dallas. Of course, the move angered Biberman and Labaudt. They were disappointed that Rowan had buckled under political pressure. In a thoughtful, measured response to his commission cancellation, Biberman took Rowan to task, suggesting that the Section's decision created a dangerous precedent that would harm the Section in the future. Withdrawal of appointments would ruin the confidence of artists and make the whole program meaningless. Secondly, "a completely chauvinistic regional attitude is created if the residents of a particular section of the country can intimidate the Section of Painting and Sculpture and force it to choose artists of that region for work to be done within that region."[86]

Biberman was incensed that — after having set aside work on another, larger commission so that he could travel to Dallas at his own expense to work on sketches — he was seeing the result of that three months' effort "suddenly vanish into thin air." Finally, he pointed out: "The healthiest thing about the position of the Section of Painting and Sculpture to date has been the absence of log rolling and political intrigue. Your present decision, however, encourages Congressmen and Senators to bring pressure upon your department, not to achieve finer artistic result, but to placate voters. This can be the ruin of any intelligent and effective government collaboration in the arts, and has been the basic reason for the stigma attached to 'official art' in other countries."[87]

Nevertheless, the separate Dallas competition went forward as announced. As a consolation, the Section paid for the California artists' travel expenses and promised them commissions nearer to home.[88] In June of 1938, after making its selection, the Section announced that the winner for the Dallas competition was the widely respected artist Peter Hurd of Santa Fe, New Mexico. The Dallas artists, who thought highly of Hurd, accepted the decision. In addition to the "Pioneer Homebuilders" and "Airmail Over Texas," the Section contracted a third mural, to be titled "East Bound Mail," but its execution was postponed until the post office completed its planned expansion of the lobby to the south. The remodeling project did not take place before the Section of Fine Arts was terminated in 1943, and the third mural was never executed.

Peter Hurd thoroughly enjoyed his new role as celebrity artist. He rolled into town one winter morning in 1940. His first task was to search for a room to spend the night. "After trying with a cab driver a dozen places I landed the last room in a dirty little dump of a hotel called 'The Texan,' across from the T[erminal] A[nnex] B[uilding] where the murals are to be," Hurd wrote to his wife Henriette at home in Santa Fe. The life of a post office mural artist was not easy, but it did have its perks. Hurd received a warm welcome on his first day on the job. "Up early this morning interviewing plasterers — etc. and found the head custodian Mr. Beverley to be most pleasant and accommodating. He allowed me keys to the building and a fine large work room close by the panels; — in the basement directly below. Here he has established for me a large roll top desk (complete with key) and I feel like a terrific big shot in 'the Department.' All lots of fun and very exciting."[89] Along with the desk, Hurd also was provided a swivel chair, "giving me for the first time in my life a tycoon feeling!"[90]

Soon, however, the long, tedious work hours began. Hurd admitted, "I feel like Quasimodo living entirely within this building. . . . A cafeteria on the mezzanine makes my leaving unnecessary for any purpose except sleeping and during the norther I even did that on my old ranch bed roll here in my workroom."[91] By February he was both working and sleeping there daily.

Like Tom Lea and other Section muralists, Hurd often worked ten-hour days, sometimes longer. Once, he reported working on his Dallas fresco from 5:30 A.M. to 11 P.M. Newspapers picked up on Hurd's unusual working and living habits and made him into a minor celebrity and a "man of mystery" who became somewhat in demand by "Dallas hostesses." He reported to his wife, however, that he had not "succumbed to any dinner dates."[92] Instead, he and his helper Ernesto Burciaga dined almost nightly at El Fénix, a neighborhood Mexican restaurant. Patrons there and other places in Dallas frequently recognized the artist from his photographs in the local newspaper.[93]

Decatur

"Texas Plains"

Ray Strong

Unavailable for viewing

3′ × 10′

Oil on canvas

1939

$800

Good condition

The ranching subject allowed Ray Strong to express the vastness of the Texas plains in this landscape mural for the Decatur post office. In the mural, a lone cowboy on horseback watches over his cattle as he contemplates the seemingly endless, rolling landscape. The sky's puffy, cumulous clouds, rhythmically spaced, recede into the horizon to create depth. The artist selected his subject with the public in mind: "From contact with the western country and small town folk I know they prefer a decoration with a living quality rather than too formal a decorative treatment of the space. The herd of beef will suggest a major industry of Texas, but my immediate concern about the design was to open up the small Post office lobby and give the person viewing it a sense of great space, sunlight and air."[94]

The former post office building at 106 South Trinity Street is now owned by the U.S. General Services Administration. It was vacant in 2003, its fate uncertain.

Eastland

"Indian Buffalo Hunt"

Suzanne Scheuer
Former Post Office
411 West Main Street
5′ × 12′
Oil on canvas
1938
$650
Good condition

This was one of two post office murals in Texas (see Caldwell entry) painted by Suzanne Scheuer. For both murals, she selected the American Indian as her subject. Scheuer respected the American Indian's freedom and nobility, and her murals pay tribute to Plains Indians' masterful horsemanship and hunting skill. The Eastland post office mural portrays two Indian hunters on horseback taking down a pair of galloping buffaloes. In the foreground, one of the mortally wounded buffaloes, an arrow in its side, crashes headlong to the ground. The other buffalo is about to meet a similar end, as the second hunter is poised to plunge his spear into his victim's side. In the background, pairs of buffaloes are pictured stampeding to safety.

An outspoken critic of the unjust way Native Americans were treated historically, Scheuer remarked: "I think it is well for us to be reminded at times of these people that have so speedily been cleared away from their territory to make room for the 'superior' white man."[95]

In a lighter vein, Scheuer included in the painting a reference to a local legend that she knew would not be lost on Eastland residents. In the lower right corner of the mural, a Texas horned "toad" watches the hunting action sleepily. According to legend, builders of the 1896 county courthouse placed a lizard and other artifacts, including a Bible and a bottle of whiskey, in the cornerstone. Thirty-one years later, in 1927, when the building was torn down, a public ceremony to open the cornerstone drew a crowd of three thousand. Officials opened the cornerstone and pulled out the contents one by one. The last thing to come out was the now dusty lizard, which the master of ceremonies held up by the tail and waved before the crowd. Suddenly, as the story goes, the creature began to twitch. It was alive! The crowd roared with excitement.[96] The lizard became an instant celebrity, and the community made Ol' Rip, as they named the creature, its mascot. Ol' Rip later paid a visit to President Calvin Coolidge in Washington and drew a smile from the chief executive.[97] Alas, Ol' Rip was not up for all the excitement. He reportedly died in 1929 of pneumonia. Eastland residents decided to keep the tangible memory of their mascot intact. City officials had the reptile embalmed, and his carcass was laid to rest in a satin-lined, open coffin where it was displayed in a glass case in the new courthouse.[98] Today, Ol' Rip's legend continues. Postcards that carry his image and narrate his story are commonly available. Visitors still pay their respects, and an annual February commemoration includes a pledge and short prayer ceremony.

Edinburg

"Harvest of the Rio Grande"

Ward Lockwood

Unavailable for viewing

4'3" × 13'

Oil on canvas

1940

$870

Destroyed, circumstances unknown

Ward Lockwood was establishing the art department at the University of Texas at Austin in the fall of 1938 when he painted the Edinburg post office mural. A visit to the lower Rio Grande valley left no doubt in his mind that agricultural abundance would be an apt subject for Edinburg. But how to express it in an interesting way? He relied on his observation of a common sight in the region. "All over Texas," he noted, "there are open-air fruit stands under awnings which are very beautiful and very colorful . . . . In these fruit stands one finds all the abundance of produce which is raised near Edinburg: oranges, grapefruit, lemons, egg plant, all sorts of vegetables, etc."[99] For the center of interest, the artist painted a young woman with long hair, wearing a long, flowing dress, and a colorful array of produce surrounding her at a roadside stand. The symbol of abundance, she cradles fruit in her lap and hands.

People of the area loved Lockwood's mural, and spectators traveled from as far as a hundred miles away to admire it. Lockwood's success in capturing the flavor of the Rio Grande valley became evident in the simple reactions of the humblest observers. According to Inslee A. Hopper, consultant to the Section chief, who happened to be visiting Edinburg, "It is the only painting in town, and even the flea-bitten, bow-legged cow hands say, 'Wal, now, that's not bad 'tall — really looks like these here parts.'"[100] Once out-of-town visitors saw the mural, the postmaster observed, their admiration changed to envy and compelled them to want a mural for their own communities.[101]

El Campo

"Rural Texas Gulf Coast"

James Milford Zornes
Post Office
110 South Mechanic Street
5′5″ × 12′
Oil on canvas
1939
$670
Restored in 1984

In this idyllic landscape of the El Campo area, white-barked trees stand like temple pillars on either side of the picture to frame a lush rural scene. Milford Zornes cleverly incorporated the postmaster's doorway into the mural, as post office mural artists often did in order to include more detail in their pictures. Zornes's mural includes much subtle action that is not obvious at first glance.

Zornes wanted to create "a glorified picture map" of the locality. "This approach," he announced, "will have more meaning to the citizens than any less graffic [*sic*] scheme. I will try to convey in it a feeling for the landscape and the atmosphere of the land. My problem is, I feel, to tell a simple story of what the people do and at the same time in an unobtrusive way give these Texans some of the poetry that they have and that they will recognize if I get it."[102]

Among the most distinctive elements in the mural are the cumulous clouds that taper off into the distance above the field and the barn, giving the mural perspective. A stream runs through the foreground, center, and beyond it a herd of cattle saunters in a clearing. A lone farmer tills his field with a horse-drawn plow. On the horizon, a barn forms the picture's central vanishing point. A road on the right passes over a bridge and extends to the distance along the growing field then passes the white farm house. In the

right, foreground, another house, older and unpainted, stands next to the stream. In the left, foreground, beneath a dense canopy of trees, a mother and child walk down a path toward the stream. Just beyond them workers sow seeds in a newly plowed field; above the trees a white bird flutters skyward. Overall, the idyllic picture renders the region a rediscovered Eden located in the Gulf Coast region of Texas.

Despite Zornes's optimism, some local residents believed that the picture did not resemble the area's landscape. Some people were dissatisfied with it, even if it were Eden. The postmaster, for example, called the mural a disappointment, complaining: "Mr. Zornes made kodak shots of our famous Bramah [sic] cattle, oil fields and sulphur mines with blocks of sulphur of approximately one million tons, . . . what we got is a combination of trees from Maine, with agriculture from Kansas."[103] Yet, this reaction seemed to reflect only a minority opinion, for the people of El Campo generally liked the mural. The postmaster capitulated, reporting grudgingly: "The expressions from the customers are that the Mural is beautiful and I recommend that it be accepted and the case closed."[104]

In 1963, when the post office was renovated, the mural was removed and stored in the basement for more than twenty years. During that time, the canvas developed dents and creases from being folded, and much of its back retained the wall plaster and lead-based glue that once held the painting on the wall. Conservators had to use scalpels to remove these encrustations when they restored the mural in 1986. Postmistress Betty Warn led a local campaign to raise the funds for the restoration.[105]

Electra

"Cattle," "Oil," and "Wheat" (three panels)

Allie Tennant

Post Office

200 West Cleveland Avenue

"Oil" (center panel)—3′3″ × 4′; "Cattle" and "Wheat"
(side panels)—4′3″ × 1′9″ each

Plaster relief

1940

$750

Cracked

A Section of Fine Arts press release tells the story of the
artist's intentions to portray the harmonious development
of Electra: "Before the discovery of oil, Electra, Texas was
devoted principally to the raising of cattle and wheat. After
that discovery, derricks and storage tanks sprang up like
mushrooms almost over night, and it is now practically im-
possible to look in any direction without seeing a tank
or a derrick." A committee composed of chamber of commerce members and the postmaster had decided on the
subject for the Electra post office mural and relayed the
idea to Dallas artist Allie Tennant on her visit to Electra in
June, 1939.[106] Looking over the rolling prairies, the artist
saw large herds of cattle and scores of wheat fields. She
concluded that the oil industry was not replacing the traditional cattle and the wheat industries. "[Oil] . . . was
simply taking its place alongside agriculture and ranching,
and there would be cattle on the plains long after the oil
was exhausted. For that reason, the artist included derricks
and tanks in all three panels, stressing oil in the center and
cattle and wheat on either side."[107]

In the left panel, a cowboy on horseback drives a herd
of white-face cattle. An oil derrick and holding tanks in the
background complete the scene in this panel and form a
backdrop in the other two, as well. The center panel concentrates on the oil industry, as three oil workers in overalls examine a set of blueprints. The right panel concentrates on agriculture, portraying a worker who carries a
sheaf of wheat under his left arm and a pitchfork in his
right hand.

Elgin

"Texas Farm"

Julius Woeltz

Post Office

21 North Avenue C

6′8″ × 12′

Oil on canvas

1940

$700

Good condition

Julius Woeltz selected a subject — work and the abundance of food — of natural interest to the people of Elgin. Woeltz wanted to portray the essential agricultural activities of the small community about thirty miles east of Austin region. Farming there was dedicated mainly to the production of grain and feed crops. The mural portrays various workers tending harvested wheat, hand-picking corn, and pitching cut grain into stacks. In the background, one worker manages a threshing machine in preparation to store the grain in a nearby elevator; a barn, water tower, and windmill appear in a cluster behind him. A crop of sunflowers frames a large, white rooster overseeing six white leghorn hens. The whole scene, thus, represents an impression of thriving and abundance on a small scale.

Woeltz explained his design to the Section this way: "The farms are usually small and production is at a slower pace than that of larger more fully mechanized areas. Therefore, I have endeavored to show the simplicity of the local activities by eliminating all but the essential subject matter."[108] Compare this simplicity that focuses on individual labor to Woeltz's compelling designs for his Amarillo commission. In that post office mural, his close-up portrayals of gang plow and disk harrow carving through the soil completely fill the canvas, stressing the mechanization of agriculture.

El Paso

"Pass of the North" (two panels plus inscription)
Tom Lea
J. Marvin Jones Federal Building
205 East Fifth Street
Two panels — 11′ × 21′ each
Oil on canvas
1938
$3,700
Good condition

Judges chose Tom Lea's design for the El Paso mural over those of forty-seven other artists.[109] The regional competition was open to artists from Arizona, Arkansas, Colorado, Kansas, Louisiana, New Mexico, Oklahoma, and Texas. In his two murals, Lea portrayed the history and development of El Paso. The murals, which hang on either side of the doorway of the post office foyer, depict early explorers and settlers of the region. The rugged landscape of arid West Texas provides the setting for these time-conflating montages. In the left panel, the sixteenth-century Spanish explorer Coronado leads the procession of conquistadors moving through the region. Clad in full armor, Coronado stands alertly beside his horse and looks hopefully into the distance. Lea also included numerous details that reflect

the natural flora and fauna characteristic of the region, such as a rattlesnake near a clump of prickly pear cactus. Also part of the Spanish expedition is a Franciscan, dressed in robe and hood and grasping his wooden cross with missionary zeal. To his left, a fully outfitted *vaquero* peers forth from a later period of El Paso's development. In the left of this panel, which suggests a succeeding period of exploration of the Southwest, a mounted ranger in full gallop charges ahead and points forward; the U.S. flag flies prominently beside him.

In the second panel of the pair, Lea arranged the details of settlement chronologically, left to right, beginning with the portrayal of two armed Apache scouts picking up clues from the trail. The mural progresses in time to a frontier couple standing together in the desolate wilderness; the settlers' resolute expression shows them to be braced for any adventure. The male figure, rifle in hand, stands ready for danger, while his bare-headed mate holds his arm in solidarity as she looks confidently into the distance. Farther to the right, a mounted cowboy in chaps and spurs scans the valley, and a wiry old miner, with determined, coal black eyes, holds a pick over one shoulder as he leads his mule. Finally, a lawman figure stands on the boardwalk of a young El Paso to symbolize the coming of law and order in the frontier settlement.

Lea's exuberance for authenticity in these murals for his home town topped that of perhaps any other Texas post office mural artist. He spent five months on the preliminary studies, painstakingly researching and capturing all the right details.[110] When he drew, he insisted on having the real articles before him. For example, he drove more than a thousand miles to Hollywood, California, to bring back to El Paso a rented replica of a conquistador's sixteenth-century attire, including morion, cuirass, jack, puffed-trunk breeches, boots, metal armor, and rapier.[111] "Everything must be true and completely understood," Lea offered, to justify his efforts.[112] He then persuaded a friend to model the full conquistador outfit while he sketched the figure standing in the blazing Texas sun. Lea described the situation: "We were working out in the sun, and the armor would get so hot you couldn't touch it — it was July — out on a sand flat." He recounted, with obvious delight, how the drops of sweat falling from the model's beard sizzled as they hit the hot armor breast plate.[113]

Lea's enthusiasm carried over to other pictorial details. He had studied various horse breeds at a friend's ranch. "Perhaps you noticed," he boasted to Rowan, "my design had four breeds of horses in it — a Palomino Spanish Barb, a cavalry Morgan, a couple of Appaloosa in-bred mustangs, and a bred-up cowpony."[114] For the friar figure, the artist recruited a Franciscan to pose for sketches. Lea made sure all the knots in the friar's rope cincture were properly tied, and he added a crucifix that friars of old wore when they traveled and worked among Indians. For the Mexican *vaquero* Lea relied on a model from the Charro Club of Juarez. The plainsman in buckskin carried a cap-and-ball rifle patterned on a weapon from Lea's grandfather's gun collection. Lea also studied 1880s photographs of Apaches for his portrayal of Native Americans.

The prospector's face was based on an old-timer whom the artist had convinced to sit for him. "I have seen these old desert rats with their burros many times out in the middle of nowhere," Lea noted about this character. "They can live on coffee, cornmeal and jackrabbits."[115] The depiction of buckskin breeches on the prospector was based on trousers belonging to his grandfather, who, Lea proudly noted, wore them on a survey party of the upper Missouri River in the 1860s. The sheriff figure was "based on an old photograph of Dallas Stoudenmire, first U.S. marshal in these parts, who was shot and killed on the streets of El Paso in the 90s, and is now a kind of local legendary figure of the wild days here."[116]

Above the doorway that separates the two panels, Lea painted an inscription that strongly articulates the artist's ideas about the heroic qualities of western settlers: "O Pass of the North Now the Old Giants Are Gone We Little Men Live Where Heroes Once Walked the Inviolate Earth." However idealistic and noble the sentiments of the inscription, Rowan had reservations about it. He feared that the words focused too much on past heroes to the extent that they disparaged the character and abilities of contemporary El Paso residents. Rowan expressed his objections to Lea, saying: "It is our opinion that as much strength of character and nobility of purpose is required to live the simple life of a good citizen today as was required by the pioneers though the latter had an opportunity of exhibiting their unquestioned courage and prowess."[117]

Lea, however, insisted that he understood the people of his home town well enough to know that they would certainly not misread the inscription. The visuals of his mural would work in tandem with the inscription to appeal to people's faith in heroes. Lea assured Rowan that, rather than putting down contemporaries, the inscription would raise their sights. People would identify with the values of those heroes. The artist argued further: "I tried to evoke heroes, as Homer did. Of course the first wanderers and 'pioneers' were not heroes in real life anymore than old cut-throat Odysseus was — but something beyond that 'real life' (perhaps that urge to walk the inviolate earth for newness' sake) is of an epical heroic nature; and it is that quality I hope to put not only into the figures but into the sky and earth around them."[118] Lea's cogent arguments convinced Section administrators to allow the use of his original inscription.

Farmersville

"Soil Conservation in Collin County"

Jerry Bywaters
Post Office
203 McKinney Street
6′10″ × 12′
Oil on canvas
1941
$700
Good condition

Jerry Bywaters's panorama of Collin County agriculture features the rolling landscape characteristic of an area where cotton, oats, corn, and wheat were among the region's main crops. The mural reinforced the federal government's urgings that farmers practice soil conservation techniques by strip cropping, terracing, and contour plow-

ing. Despite the obvious signs of power plowing in the mural, the artist kept images of tractors out of the picture, as the postmaster requested. The civil servant did want chickens included in his post office mural, and, as a nostalgic boon to small farms in a time of increasing mechanization, Bywaters complied. The Section of Fine Arts judges were delighted with the completed work, considering it well thought out and designed.

Bywaters's reputation as a regionalist and a muralist did not go unrecognized. He had previously worked on the Dallas City Hall historical mural sequence (now destroyed) for the Public Works of Art Project, the mural program immediately preceding the Section of Fine Arts. Rowan, who knew Bywaters's work from several other federal murals, including those in Houston, Quanah, and Trinity, acknowledged the "quality of great dignity" of Bywaters's work and his growth as an artist.[119]

Fort Worth

"Two Texas Rangers," "The Taking of Sam Bass," and
"Flags Over Texas"

Frank Mechau

Federal Courthouse (second-floor courtroom — access
restricted)

Jennings and Lancaster Streets

"Two Texas Rangers" — 8' × 11'6"; "The Taking of Sam
Bass" — 8' × 11'6"; and "Flags Over Texas" — 5'9" × 3'8"

Oil on canvas

1940

$2,900

Good condition

The two main murals in this group, which are located on
the back wall of the circuit courtroom of the federal courthouse in downtown Fort Worth, portray two opposing
Texas folk heroes — Texas Rangers and the outlaw Sam
Bass. Rangers garnered widespread respect as keepers of
law and order in the young state.[120] Yet, outlaw Bass was
also regarded with respect; as a folk hero he possessed such
qualities as individualism and generosity, and he was a fellow of the common man. He was a Robin Hood–type of
hero who generously shared his loot after stealing it from
the rich.[121] These two figures, lawman and outlaw, were fit-
ting symbols in depression America.

Sam Bass's reputation as a Robin Hood character

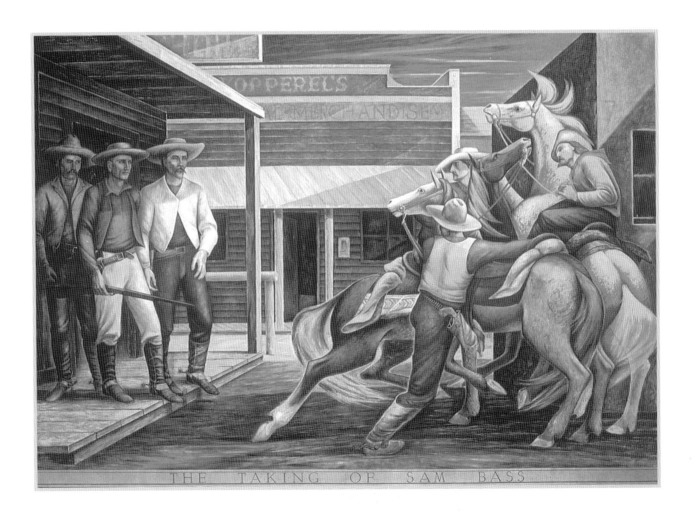

THE   TAKING   OF   SAM   BASS

partly arose from the bandit's quirky habit of reimbursing folks whenever he stole something from them during his desperate attempts to flee authorities. According to legend, Bass insisted on paying for his debts in $20 gold pieces that he had stolen in his robberies. For example, as the story goes, when Bass needed a fresh horse, he would stop some hapless traveler and politely ask for his mount. Sometimes the frightened victims would give up their horses even before being asked. But, much to the victims' astonishment, Bass would not only pay for the horse, but he often would *overpay*. Another story tells of Bass's generosity when he and his gang dropped in as uninvited guests at a rural farmhouse, causing the widow who lived there considerable trepidation. Bass insisted that his men act politely, and, the next morning, after he and his gang had enjoyed a good night's rest and a hearty breakfast, Bass left the widow the considerable sum of $50 for the inconvenience.[122]

Texas Rangers appear in the first of Mechau's mural sequence. They are working with horses at a corral when they are notified of an imminent bank robbery. In the second panel, the Rangers confront members of the Bass gang as they are about to rob a bank. The action is frozen just prior to the bloody shootout that led to Sam Bass's demise. The actual event occurred in Round Rock.

Outlaws and Texas Rangers both possess admirable qualities of folk heroes. Mechau avoided depicting a bloody gunfight, which would have been unacceptable to Section officials. Mechau's portrayals stress the dignity of both the Rangers and Sam Bass and do not demand that the viewer choose between these two worthy adversaries. Together, the murals present a fable to reinforce the concept of social order, while allowing the artist to venerate subtly the legend of Sam Bass and his popular kind of justice.[123]

In the third panel, the image of the state seal of Texas is superimposed on a flag of the Republic of Texas from 1836, which is now the state flag. A saddle, rope, spurs, a rifle, and a red bandanna surrounding the flags symbolize the state's early days.

Fredericksburg

"Loading Cattle"

Otis Dozier

Post Office

125 West Main Street

5′ × 10′

Oil on canvas

1942

$750

Good condition

Little information is available on Otis Dozier's creation of the mural about Fredericksburg's ranching industry. The Section of Fine Arts judges praised Dozier's composition highly, favoring it over his earlier designs, including one that featured angora goats, which were raised commercially in the Texas Hill Country. Rowan, however, approved the artist's sketch of Hereford cattle as more representative of the region's livestock.

The mural features the final stage in the process when cattle are shipped to market, as cowboys herd cattle from the holding pen onto a livestock railroad car. One cowboy stretches down from his horse to prod a rebellious cow, adding a sense of vigorous action to the scene. Rowan complimented Dozier's "entertaining arrangement of elements in the picture"[124] and commended the artist for the energy of his presentation and the convincing spatial relationships.[125]

Gatesville

"Off to Northern Markets"

Joe De Yong

Post Office

802 East Leon Street

5′ × 10′

Oil on canvas

1939

$670

Good condition, moved from old post office to new

Joe De Yong of Santa Barbara, California, chose a typical cattle drive as the subject of his mural for the Central Texas community of Gatesville. The artist justified his choice of subject with a historical note: "Opening of northern ranges and markets to the Texas cowman spelled economic salvation to the people of Texas."[126] In the foreground of the mural, a cook drives his chuck wagon along the trail and snaps the reins over his mule team. In the distance, cowboys are busy driving a herd of horses and a large herd of cattle. Farther in the distance, a narrow band of hills frames the expansiveness of the region.

Claiming to be an authority on cattle drives, De Yong declared that he "grew up among Texas cowmen, in Oklahoma, and know their point of view."[127] The artist worked on the Gatesville mural while he was technical adviser and costume designer for the Cecil B. De Mille movie *Union Pacific*. He worked previously on the set for De Mille's film *The Plainsman* at Paramount in 1936. De Yong also claimed the distinction of having studied with famed western artist Charles M. Russell.[128]

Giddings

"Cowboys Receiving the Mail"

Otis Dozier

Post Office

79 East Austin Street

4′ × 12′6″

Oil on canvas

1939

$670

Good condition

In the summer of 1938, Otis Dozier sent several preliminary sketches to the section for approval of an appropriate design for the Giddings post office. Of these, one sketch featured pony express riders and another portrayed cowboys receiving mail. When Dozier traveled to Giddings he discovered that cowboys there were scarce.[129] The postmaster proudly informed him that the town instead had one of the largest poultry processing plants in the region.

Dozier prepared some sketches of the poultry business and submitted them for section approval. That unsavory subject, however, did not fit with the Section's goal to supply the public with works of beauty.[130] Rowan, instead, encouraged Dozier to pursue his sketch of cowboys receiving the mail, which he considered a charming design that also emphasized the mail's importance in people's lives. In the mural, cowboys gather around a rural mailbox as one of them excitedly opens his newly arrived parcel, which contains a pair of red cowboy dress boots. A second cowboy nearby eagerly reads a letter that he has received, while a third cowboy stands apart on horseback and looks on in disappointment at not having received mail. Dozier's finished mural includes a mountain in the background, although Giddings's actual terrain is completely flat. Still, despite this error and the lack of cowboys in Giddings, the community liked the mural, and the postmaster dubbed it a "first class job."[131]

Graham

"Oil Fields of Graham"

Alexandre Hogue

Young County Historical Museum (former post office)

510 Third Street

$7' \times 12'$

Oil on canvas

1939

$550

Restored, in good condition

This mural by Texas regionalist Alexandre Hogue features the general theme of work. Hogue selected the oil industry as his subject, stressing the motifs of progress and prosperity. In the montage, a welder in overalls and goggles straddles a segment of pipeline as he and an assistant make a weld to join two sections. A state-of-the-art "two-way" pump and a new tanker truck loom conspicuously in the immediate background. The field boss and an executive read a blueprint together on one side of the painting; the figure on the right bears the likeness of the Graham postmaster, Boyd Street, whom the artist used as his model.[132] On the left, detached from the scene, stands an old man — a portrait of the the town's founder, E. S. Graham. Wearing nineteenth-century attire, he gazes aloofly past the main activity. In the background, behind old man Graham, stand oil rigs, tanks, boilers, derricks, and other machinery associated with oil production.

Section officials criticized Hogue's prominent placement of the town patriarch. Rowan asserted that Graham looked too stiff and detached.[133] He observed, further, that the figure had a "rather heavy and forbidding" appearance. As a remedy, Rowan called for this and the other figures in the mural to be "more interesting to the people who visit the Post Office."[134] Hogue briskly defended his E. S. Graham figure: "This man *was* stiff and lived in a *stiff age*, long before oil was discovered and so I know what the people would say should I have him taking part in activities of which he was not a part." The Section had also deemed the two figures to the right uninteresting. To this the artist replied, "The two men I have used represent a field foreman getting instructions from a district superintendent, a figure who represents the business end of oil. Anyone in Graham will know who they are supposed to be." Hogue defiantly refused to sign the contract until the Section saw things his way.[135]

Section leaders wished to be perceived as champions of democracy in their support of artistic freedom. Here was a test. Rowan assured Hogue that his suggestions were not intended to violate that freedom but to improve the mural. "You must realize by now," Rowan reminded Hogue, "that the purpose of the Section is not to hold back an artist but to give him as much encouragement and assistance as possible."[136] The Section ultimately accepted Hogue's initial design.

Hogue completed the mural in the spacious study of his good friend, Dallas artist Jerry Bywaters, by January, 1939. Prior to its installation, Hogue displayed the canvas for two weeks in a one-man exhibition at the Hockaday School in Dallas, where he was an instructor.[137] In the 1980s, the U.S. Postal Service sold the post office building to the City of Graham, which turned it over to local citizens to use as a historical museum.

Hamilton

"Texas Rangers in Camp"

Ward Lockwood

Post Office

120 South Rice Street

5'9" × 11'

Fresco secco (tempera on dry plaster)

1942

$800

Flaking, fragile

The *Hamilton County News* announced, "An amazingly interesting and intrigueing [*sic*] scene has been developing from day to day on the portion of the walls directly above the door of the private office of Postmaster George H. Boynton."[138] In his mural for the Hamilton post office, Ward Lockwood portrayed a group of Texas Rangers relaxing around their campfire at night. One of them plays a fiddle, one plays a guitar, one sings, and a fourth enjoys the music as he cleans his carbine. The *Hamilton Herald Record* raved about the mural: "Every Hamiltonian and every Texan who's ever read a book, seen a movie, or listened to the tales their grandfathers told can appreciate 'Texas Rangers in Camp' . . . . even a Texas Ranger himself could appreciate Lockwood's art!"[139] The artist was tickled at the enthusiasm among spectators for his mural: "From the spontaneous remarks of visitors in the Post Office I am sure that the mural is the most popular one I have done."[140] Although the mural was restored in 1991, it continues to deteriorate, due, partly, to fluctuations in the lobby's climate.[141] Texas Rangers appear as the focus of several Section murals, including those in Fort Worth, Mission, and Smithville.

Henderson

"Local Industries"
Paul Ninas
Unavailable for viewing
6′ × 12′6″
Fresco
1937
$650
Destroyed, painted over in the 1950s[142]

The post office mural for Henderson portrays activities from the community's principal industries. In one section of the painting, Paul Ninas represented a group of men engrossed in various agricultural tasks, including shouldering sacks of corn and moving a bale of cotton on a hand truck. To the right, in the distance, the plowed furrows carved into the soil create a symmetrical pattern on the distant hill. In the foreground, a single corn plant symbolizes that crop's importance to Henderson. The oil industry is represented with numerous oil derricks receding into the distance. Ninas prominently included the latest model of airplane — a symbol of progress that appeared in many post office murals and in other public art of the period.

Ninas worked on the preliminary sketches at his New Orleans studio before attempting the full-size drawing, or cartoon. The artist's progress was delayed while he implemented Rowan's suggestions to improve the arrangement and scale of the workers in order to create the illusion of more depth.[143] The changes, together with bureaucratic delays in payment, caused the artist to doubt whether he could proceed, due to lack of funds.[144] Similar delays affected other section mural artists whose careers were not established before the depression and who had relatively few outlets for their art. After Ninas completed the full-size cartoon for his fresco, he sent a photo of it to Rowan, explaining why it was six inches shorter than the post office blueprint's specified measurement — the artist's drawing board was only twelve feet long. Ninas added the missing elements when he traveled to Henderson to paint the mural.[145]

Hereford

"On the Range"

Enid Bell

Post Office

408 North Main Street

6′11″ × 4′2″

Relief carving, polychrome wood (white pine)

1941

$730

Good condition

Enid Bell captured the myth of the cowboy in her polychrome wood carving, "On the Range," for the Hereford post office. A team of cowhands relaxes around a campfire; one of them strums his guitar while another plays the harmonica. Two other cowhands recline, listening.[146] Bell gracefully portrays the close relationship between cowboys and their cattle by having one cow curve from behind the harmonica player and dip its head to drink from the nearby watering hole. A saguaro cactus protrudes from behind the cow. Although the saguaro adds a western flavor

to the piece, it seems to betray the artist's misconception about or disregard for the actual landscape of Texas. Similar anomalies occur in Thomas Stell's mural for the Teague post office, suggesting that at least some artists played up stereotypes of the West.

Bell executed the 150-pound sculpture in white pine at her Santa Fe, New Mexico, workshop. The public responded to her artwork enthusiastically. The postmaster praised it, saying: "We are truly grateful for this fine piece of art which typifies and perpetuates the spirit of an era that has contributed so much to the lives and culture of this section of the United States."[147] The artist reported at the time of the mural's installation that one lone cowboy, upon viewing the work, exclaimed that it was "a mighty fine piece of whittling."[148] Inslee Hopper, assistant to the Section of Fine Arts chief, complimented the artist by noting: "When your work appeals to the cowboys as whittling and to the Section as sculpture and to the postmaster as an historical record, I think you have really accomplished something."[149]

The sculpture suffered a streak of ill luck during building remodeling in 1967. A contractor took the piece from the post office wall and, claiming he had salvage rights over the work, installed it above the fireplace of his Dallas residence.[150] After the U.S. General Services Administration became custodian of the facility and its artwork, officials tracked down the contractor and retrieved the sculpture. The GSA did not, however, reinstall the artwork in the remodeled post office, opting to store it in a Fort Worth warehouse for several years. The GSA allegedly refused repeated requests by Hereford's postmaster to loan the sculpture to the Deaf Smith County Museum in Hereford. However, in 1973, through the intervention of U.S. Senator Ralph W. Yarborough, the GSA returned it to the Hereford post office.[151] Yet another incident threatened survival of the woodcarving in 1985, when a painting contractor accidentally knocked the sculpture from the wall. The work split into sections, but, fortunately, the worker managed to reassemble the pieces with carpenter's glue.[152]

Houston

"Houston Ship Canal—Early History" (two panels by Alexandre Hogue): "Construction of the Canal" and "The *Diana* Docking"

"Houston Ship Canal—Contemporary Scenes" (three panels by Jerry Bywaters): "Loading Cotton," "Loading Oil," and "Ship Turning Basin (Aerial View)"

Bob Casey Federal Building and U.S. Courthouse

515 Rusk Avenue

"Construction of the Canal"—6′6″ × 6′6″; "The *Diana* Docking"—6′6″ × 6′6″; "Loading Cotton"—6′6″ × 6′6″; "Loading Oil"—6′6″ × 6′6″; and "Ship Turning Basin (Aerial View)"—5′6″ × 2′6″

Oil on canvas

1941

$1,300 (each artist)

Good condition

Dallas artists and close friends Jerry Bywaters and Alexandre Hogue created this group of murals for the now-demolished Houston Parcel Post Building at 500 Washington Avenue. The panels present historical, developmental, and progressive themes through subjects of work and industry. Bywaters and Hogue shared the commission, awarded them based on their submissions for the Dallas post office mural competition. For this project, the artists chose to depict one of the most significant events in Houston's development: the Houston ship channel was transforming the city into the major Texas port.

The artists flipped a coin to determine which panels each would paint. It fell to Hogue to paint the channel's history.[153] In "Houston Ship Canal—Early History," Hogue portrays the surveying and dredging operation of the 1910 federally funded project. Hogue's second, related mural presents the artist's imaginative interpretation of the bustle of activity on the wharf after the channel's completion. In it, the steamboat *Diana* sits docked at Houston's Buffalo Bayou to "wood up" and board passengers and cargo.[154] The wooden Indian and the sheriff that dominate

the foreground, Hogue explained, were a common sight in such wharf settings. Hogue exercised his artistic license by including, anachronistically, some historically significant buildings in the mural's background. The large building on the far bank of the channel represents a hotel that served as the Texas capitol when Sam Houston was president of the Republic of Texas from 1837. The log cabin in the background represents one of Sam Houston's law offices.[155]

One of Bywaters's three panels characterizes a contemporary wharf scene where teamsters load bales of cotton onto a freighter. In his second panel, workers operate the control valves prior to transferring crude oil from a pipeline to the tanker. Bywaters in addition painted a map of the ship channel showing the turning basin and the

location of the wharves. After reporters covered the artists at work, Hogue quipped cynically that the newspapers "sent photographers to 'get us in action,' mostly rubbing lead out of our eyes."[156] Lead was commonly present in the glue used to attach mural canvases to the wall.

In 1962, the postmaster removed the murals and placed them in storage before the wrecking ball razed the Parcel Post Building. The paintings were forgotten until 1975, when a General Services Administration district manager found them rolled up and hidden beneath a pile of electrical equipment in a Houston GSA warehouse.

John O'Neill, a faculty member of the art and art history department at Rice University, had initiated the search for the murals.[157] The artworks were displayed in an exhibit at Rice University before they were placed in the new Bob Casey Federal Building downtown.[158]

At the time of the murals' rediscovery, Bywaters was asked to comment on the artistic freedom of those working on commission for the federal government's mural program. "There was no censorship," Bywaters said, "but it helped if you boned up a little on local history before you submitted an idea for a competition."[159]

Houston

"Travis' Letter from the Alamo" and "Sam Houston's Report on the Battle of San Jacinto"

William McVey
Unavailable for viewing
4'6" × 5' each
Relief sculptures in Tymstone (cast stone)
1941
$1,440
Lost

The Section of Fine Arts designated a second Houston post office as a mural site and awarded the job to William McVey, a Texas sculptor.[160] According to McVey, his subject involved "the two most important letters in Texas history — Travis' letter from the Alamo (a plea for aid the day before the battle) and Sam Houston's laconic report on the San Jacinto rout."[161] McVey had recently joined the faculty of the University of Texas at Austin when he received the commission for his pair of sculptures. His sketch of the panels called for bold planes to compensate for the poor

light in the building.[162] Yet the artist was in a quandary about the appropriate material to use for the composition. He ruled out several choices, including his favored and the very trendy choice of aluminum. At a cost of $500 per panel, aluminum was much too expensive for his modest budget.[163] He also rejected wood. Plaster was a possibility, but McVey was not enthusiastic about the weight of the medium. He sought the Section's guidance regarding the medium.[164] Inslee Hopper, assistant to the Section chief, suggested a new material called Tymstone, which had been developed by Michael Tym of Chicago. Tymstone was lighter than plaster and had the handsome green color of oxidized copper, as in antique bronze.[165] Each Tymstone panel would cost about $60, which made it an attractively affordable choice of material.[166] McVey sculpted the clay models for the casting molds for the Tymstone and was pleased with the results. Each sculpture weighed 120 pounds. Unfortunately, the works have been lost. No trace of them can be found in the federal building on LaBranch Street.

Jasper

"Industries of Jasper"

Alexander Levin

New Post Office

217 North Bowie Street

5′ × 13′

Oil on canvas

1939

$560

Restored in 1988, transferred to new post office

During the summer of 1938, Alexander Levin traveled from his home in Los Angeles to Jasper. Once there, the postmistress and other citizens assisted him in selecting the lumber industry as his mural subject. In the artist's words, "I tried to design the mural for the Post Office so that it can be thought of as a monument to the people who through this industry participated in the building up of the Jasper community."[167]

Levin's tribute to the pre-mechanized East Texas lumber industry focuses on the vigorous manual labor of several workers engaged in lumber-related tasks. The setting is a lumber camp in the Piney Woods of East Texas. Levin's depiction of shirtless lumberjacks vigorously sawing a log acknowledges the industriousness of the people in utilizing the raw resources at hand to their advantage. The dynamic action of the middle ground shows two men struggling to load logs on a flat-bed truck: one of the men prods the team of straining horses. In the background, carpenters, busily constructing a wood-frame house, represent a trade derived from the lumber industry. Cattle graze in the background to signify other work opportunities that developed after trees had been clear-cut. In the distance, a locomotive chugs through the countryside to suggest future economic development for the area.

Kaufman

"Driving the Steers"

Margaret A. Dobson

Unavailable for viewing

4'10" × 12'

Oil on canvas

1939

$560

Destroyed c. 1976

Margaret A. Dobson received the commission for the Kaufman post office mural based on the quality of her design entry for the Dallas Parcel Post Building competition. She chose a traditional cattle drive as her subject over a representation of Kaufman's oil industry because, she reasoned, the oil-drilling apparatus would soon appear outdated.[168] In addition, a traditional cattle drive would be a more stable subject and technically easier to research without requiring her to make a special trip to Kaufman to make study sketches. The price of a round-trip train ticket from Dobson's home in Santa Monica, California, which cost $79.30 at the time, made her balk. It was an expense that she believed was disproportionate to her small stipend for the mural.[169]

The perspective of Dobson's skillful mural design leads the viewer directly into this western scene. Three cowboys on horseback herding cattle move diagonally from the central left toward the lower right foreground. One of the cowboys dominates the left foreground with a black-and-white dog running excitedly alongside the horse. The Kaufman postmaster reported in the early 1980s that, when the plaster on which the mural was glued began to fall off the wall (and the painting along with it), the postmaster at the time (1976) had the mural removed and discarded and the vacant wall covered with paneling.[170] The mural image reproduced here is taken from the artist's original black-and-white photograph, which is now held in the National Archives.[171]

Kenedy

"Grist for the Mill"
Charles Campbell
Post Office
223 South Second Street
6′ × 14′
Oil on canvas
1939
$560
Good condition

Charles Campbell's mural of the cotton harvest in Kenedy features two male figures shouldering their sacks stuffed with cotton. A female worker drags her sack of picked cotton from the field for weighing prior to the contents being fed into the gin. A male figure sits at the edge of the bin and with his legs directs the cotton toward the vacuum that is operated by an African American figure. The artist

effectively captures the expression of weariness on the workers' faces.

Campbell's amusing account of his attempt to find an appropriate historical subject illustrates the way some mural subjects were selected. At the suggestion of the Section of Fine Arts, Campbell, who was living in Castroville (about thirty miles east of San Antonio), dutifully made a trip to Kenedy to research the region.

The Section encouraged artists to choose historical subjects, because they would inspire people. "I finally . . . unearthed the fact that Kenedian history is a history of some of the bloodier gunfights[,] that Kenedy was known as Six-shooter Junction[,] and it occasionally was still so announced, jokingly, by the bus driver." People would normally be thrilled to see their community's history portrayed on the post office wall. But, as Campbell discovered, some Kenedy residents were not fond of displaying their violent past publicly. Meeting with Kenedy's postmaster and the

unofficial town historian, Campbell probed for a key moment of Kenedy's past, but his effort proved an embarrassment. "I put out a few cautious feelers," he related, "as to the reception of a panel depicting a good juicy bang-up, old-fashioned gun squabble to immortalize the glamorous past-aliveness. The [town's] historian . . . cast down his eyes and gave me a reproachful glance and a small deprecatory laugh. The Postmaster coughed politely and said, 'Well, we'd rather kind of forget all that. That's not the sort of thing we want to keep before the public.'"[172]

Campbell then turned instead to local industry for a mural subject and found it in cotton. With the postmaster as his guide, the artist toured the cotton seed oil mills, the gins, the warehouses, and the compressors and observed them in full operation. "I found the cotton industry is the life of the place," Campbell noted. "Without cotton there would be no Kenedy. And even were there other sources of livelihood, I should still have concentrated on the cotton industry for it impressed me more strongly than anything I have seen for some time."[173] The artist reported that he was especially taken by "the tremendous aliveness of the men working under such conditions."[174]

Despite Campbell's lively attempt to pay tribute to the central role of cotton to Kenedy, the artist's preliminary sketch lacked political correctness, according to the Section. Rowan suggested that the artist create an ethnic balance that would be better in line with what he perceived were local biases. "One of the questions which arises in our minds in relation to the decoration of Federal buildings, particularly in the South," Rowan cautioned, "is the reaction of the people to a decoration exclusively stressing Negro activities."[175] Campbell told Rowan that the postmaster was well aware that all mill labor was African American except for the overseers, and that the workforce was divided equally between Mexicans and African Americans in the field. The artist further reassured Rowan that the postmaster was certain that anything Campbell painted about the industry would please the people. Nevertheless, Rowan insisted on more non–African American workers, and Campbell complied, with one exception. Responding sardonically, he wrote: "For the sake of authenticity, I hope the one Negro will be permitted to remain."[176] The Section conceded.

Kilgore

"Drilling for Oil," "Pioneer Saga," "Music of the Plains," and "Contemporary Youth" (four panels)

Post Office

200 South Kilgore Street

Xavier Gonzalez

"Drilling for Oil"—5′10½″ × 16′7½″; "Pioneer Saga"—

5′10½″ × 16′7½″; "Music of the Plains"—6′ × 4′; and

"Contemporary Youth"—6′ × 4′

Oil on canvas

1941

$2,600

Restored[177]

Exploration and development are the general themes that unify Kilgore's four post office murals, with subjects ranging from pioneer settlers to oil exploration to social life. The assumption underlying the murals is the belief in progress arising from the spirit of adventure and from hard work. The two large murals that dominate the spacious Kilgore post office lobby establish the exploration theme; two smaller, related murals complement them. One of the two large murals, "Pioneer Saga," which is located above the postmaster's door, offers a romantic view of a group of travel-weary pioneers stopping for refreshment at a stream. The blonde-haired patriarch holding his musket peers intently beyond the picture's frame. The young boy places his hand trustingly on the Indian scout's shoulder as he looks toward the father. The gesture implies the social bonds between generations and between races. The Madonna-like figure of this frontier holy family is pictured in the foreground bathing her young child. In the background another female figure sitting at the front of the covered wagon suckles her infant. The oxen drinking from the stream adds to this idyllic picture. Other male figures perform various tasks. On the opposite wall, strategically facing "Pioneer Saga," the companion mural, "Drilling for Oil," represents a leap in time from pioneer days into the modern era. The juxtaposition implies that hard work brings progress and wealth. Kilgore, of course, became the center of the 1930s East Texas oil boom after Columbus Marion "Dad" Joiner struck a vast oil reserve nearby. A federal bulletin describes the mural's depiction of the "moment when the pipe has gone its whole length and the

drills and crew of rough-necks are ready to raise the pipe and to insert another to the rotary unit. . . . On the left is day. On the right is night to indicate the continuity of work uninterrupted until its completion."[178]

The theme of exploration also extends to the development of culture on the western frontier, which the vignettes of the smaller panels, "Music of the Plains" and "Contemporary Youth," illustrate. In "Music of the Plains," a female singer croons beside her accompanist who strums a guitar. The duo seems to represent the development of individual talent in the tradition of Texas folk music. The vignette in a second small panel suggests the exploration of new social roles represented by another young couple dressed up as for a prom and waltzing romantically together. In the background of this mural, a youngster plays with a model plane as if to fly it. He seems to be exploring his future role as a pilot. The boy's model airplane is a symbol of his dreams and of the development of commercial flight. Again, in this mural, as in the others, the setting is rural Texas. The canvases of the two small murals are irregularly shaped and mounted frameless on the wall. Their undefined borders suggest the wistfulness of the subjects.

Gonzalez paid careful attention to the authenticity of details in the murals, especially in depicting the oil drilling activity. He was well aware that most local residents were knowledgeable of oil operations and would be quick to notice any inconsistency or error. Oil workers used a variety of methods and tools, which the artist observed closely and sketched on site during his research visit to Kilgore.[179] How successful was he in satisfying the local "experts"?

Kilgore residents seemed pleased with Gonzalez's results. According to a *Kilgore News Herald* article, despite the artist's missing a few technicalities, he "has ably brought most of the operation of the production phase of the oil industry into the canvas."[180] The article's additional comments also reveal popular ideas about good art and the writer's opinion of other murals he had seen. The article ridiculed those as it praised Kilgore's murals, which proved "more satisfying to the average person than most. Little distortion of perspective or subjects appears and the mural-people are not stolid, huge humans as in some popular conceptions of mural art."[181]

Because people in small communities such as Kilgore were exposed rarely to artists or original art, they showed a fascination with them that sometimes ranged from amusement to bewilderment. For the Kilgore postmaster, bewilderment turned to respect. His comments — intended as compliments — suggest that Gonzalez must be a "real artist." He went so far as to suggest that Gonzalez was a human paint brush: "He [Gonzalez] came here and went to work, getting paint over him from head to foot — including his hair when he finished, he was so engrossed in the work."[182]

La Grange

"Horses"

Tom E. Lewis

Post Office

113 East Colorado Street

4′ × 10′

Oil on canvas

1939

$660

Damaged

Little public record exists about the creation of this mural, which artist Tom Lewis originally conceived of as "Circus Horses." A Section of Fine Arts announcement described the mural merely as "a western range scene with a rhythmic design of horses and cattle in a rural setting."[183] Instead of painting a circus, the artist changed his design to reflect a rural scene, which is more appropriate to the Central Texas region where La Grange is located. Rowan generously praised Lewis's sketch as "an admirable design for a mural, . . . and a glorious thing in itself."[184]

Lamesa

"The Horse Breakers"

Fletcher Martin

Unavailable for viewing[185]

3′7″ × 13′

Oil on canvas

1939

$950

Good condition

Fletcher Martin, a Los Angeles artist, captured the movement and excitement of the moment when two cowhands attempt to saddle a bronco. One of the men firmly holds the horse's bridle and struggles to control the animal. The bronco is blindfolded, keeping the man approaching with a blanket and saddle out of its line of sight. Four other horses in the background prance nervously around the corral.

The postmaster had few good words to say about the mural when it was installed in his post office. He complained that he had expected to see more people and a few chickens. Martin's sarcastic response reflects the artist's frustration: "His [the postmaster's] passion for bucolic characters and gallinaceous bipeds might have been gratified to some degree had he replied to my requests for subject matter suggestions."[186]

Perhaps a more serious criticism than the lack of chickens, however, was the postmaster's pronouncement that certain details in the painting were not characteristic of the region where Lamesa is located and that the painting, therefore, was not authentic. For example, he scorned the type of horse the artist pictured, which he emphatically believed did not resemble horses of West Texas "now or ever before." Nor did he approve of the horsebreaker figures who, he believed, looked "like some square headed Russians or something else."[187] Finally, the disgruntled official dismissed the painting as "entirely out of line and not suitable at all to the locality," adding that the whole community would be glad if it could be changed.[188] "I would say that the work so far as I can tell is fine but the picture is 'Terrible.'"[189]

Section officials, however, refused to be cowed by the rural bureaucrat's parochialism. Inslee Hopper, consultant to the Section of Fine Arts chief, asserted to the postmaster that the painting was "designed and executed with vigor and a convincing reality."[190] He went on to point out to the postmaster that the horses were meant to be "decorative" rather than portraits of any specific breed. As for the postmaster's xenophobic comment about the shape of the characters' heads, Hopper asserted that the characters in the painting did not seem to be "any particular nationality other than American."[191] In the end, Lamesa received its mural the way Martin had painted it.

Lampasas

"Afternoon on a Texas Ranch"

Ethel Edwards
Post Office
401 East Second Street
4'6" × 12'
Oil on canvas
1941
$740
Good condition

In the era following the Dust Bowl, when the depression created widespread want, Ethel Edwards's mural for the Lampasas post office offered an alternative perspective of prosperity and serenity. The mural perpetuates the elusive myth of idyllic rural America. Edwards articulated the subject of her mural in a letter to Forbes Watson, special assistant to the chief of the Section of Fine Arts: "It is afternoon on a Texas farm. Long dark clouds are forming over the hills which grow dark against the light of the setting sun. I have attempted to give a sensation of peacefulness and rest which comes after a day of work. The animals are quiet—even windmills rest in the still air."[192]

Edwards incorporated all the elements of a nostalgic rural scene. The mural focuses on a cow and her calf standing out from the rest of the enclosed herd. The cow curls protectively around her newborn calf, licking her offspring. Pictured to the left, in another corral, a herd of horses includes a mare with her foal at her side. In the right portion of the painting, hogs forage greedily, and the central mid-distance contains a farm house, windmills, and out buildings that are set against a vast landscape with hills beyond.

In December, 1940, on the day Edwards installed her mural, crowds of people suddenly converged on the small Lampasas post office. Many of the curious visitors came from surrounding ranches just to see the mural. "The Post Office was filled with cowboys, ranchers and their families," Edwards reported, "people of the town all watching with interest. The tinker of the town told me it was the prettiest painting he'd ever seen. One little lady in black suggested I fatten up my hogs."[193] The marvelous sight rendered some onlookers speechless. "A man came in to mail a letter. When he suddenly saw what was going on, he said, 'Jesus!' and rushed out returning with his whole family asking excitedly, 'What's happening?' 'There,' he said. 'I told you I couldn't explain it to you.'" One rancher looked at the mural a long time and finally said ingenuously, "'Well, that's a pretty good imitation, yes siree!'"[194]

During Edwards's stay, Lampasas residents demonstrated their appreciation for her efforts in every small way they could. The hotel owner reduced the price of her room. The hardware store reduced the price of the brushes that the artist and her assistant used to glue the canvas to the wall. For fifty cents, the restaurant/drug store served more fried chicken than the two could eat. Edwards derived satisfaction from the attention, because it indicated that people were happy with her creation.[195]

Liberty

"The Story of the Big Fish"

Howard Fisher

New post office

1515 Sam Houston Street

5'5" × 13'10"

Oil on canvas

1939

$750

Good condition

Howard Fisher's commission for the Baytown post office was canceled due to a federal accounting error that inadvertently used up the allotted funds for that mural. Instead, he was offered the opportunity to adapt one of his sketches to fit over the postmaster's door in the new post office at Liberty, about thirty miles from Baytown. The Section compensated Fisher for his additional expense and the inconvenience with an increased payment. To portray the early fishing industry on the Gulf Coast, Fisher chose the subject of fishermen sharing "big fish" stories of their adventures. The three bare-chested sailors mending their nets on the wharf seem captivated by one old salt's yarns.

Linden

"Cotton Pickers"

Victor Arnautoff
Post Office
201 East Rusk Street
4′6″ × 10′9″
Oil on canvas
1939
$670
Good condition

In the Linden post office mural, the artist's portrayal of a cotton plantation looks back to an earlier time before machines dominated agriculture. The mural recreates the dramatic interplay of workers engaged in harvesting cotton. Three barefoot, female laborers in a field stoop to pick cotton boles as they drag their long white sacks behind them. All of the women workers are dressed in white, and their faces are hidden by their starched white bonnets. The patterns created by the white elements in the painting offer a striking contrast to the darkness of the surrounding foliage and draw the viewer's attention to the essential movement of the workers. The trailing white cotton sacks help give the impression of the toil endured by the stooped figures who seem slowed by the weight of their burden. In the middle distance, two more field hands make their way in the opposite direction through the rows of cotton. In the far distance on a hill sits the plantation owner's mansion shaded by a thick cluster of trees. Beside it, in stark contrast, stands a field hand's quarters, a mere shanty with a barren, leafless tree standing symbolically beside it.

The Linden job was Arnautoff's second mural in Texas, after College Station. The artist accepted the Linden commission so far from his home in San Francisco with ambivalence. Despite the inconvenience and travel cost, he believed that the experience of making a mural for the federal government would bring him future credibility as a professional artist.[196] Yet, it was a bitter pill for him to swallow; all his efforts left him no better off financially than before he began, and Arnautoff questioned the Section's motives for assigning murals to artists so far from their home when traveling expenses consumed such a large proportion of their payment. "I was very much pleased by your invitation to execute another mural and at the same time I was very much discouraged," Arnautoff wrote to Rowan. "I was discouraged because after I shall receive my final payment for the mural which I just completed and installed [in College Station], and after I pay all my bills connected with the said installation, there will be exactly $10 left."[197]

Rowan's only response was that few new post offices were being built in California, resulting in a lack of opportunities under the Section of Fine Arts for post office murals in that state. In any event, when Arnautoff finished the Linden mural, the citizens seemed to appreciate the artist's efforts. According to the postmaster, the painting was "an excellent piece of work admired by everyone."[198] Rowan, too, appreciated the mural's "beauty and charm"[199] and the "rhythm and dignity of the three workers."[200]

Littlefield

"West Texas"

William McVey
Lamb County offices (former post office)
110 East Sixth Street
c. 2′ × 5′
Two relief sculptures in Tymstone
1948
Price unknown
Excellent condition

These two molded stone sculptures on the wall above the postmaster's door of Littlefield's former post office portray cotton farming and ranching. Each sculpture consists of the busts of three vertically stacked figures; each character performs a task related either to ranching or agriculture. In the ranching sculpture, the top figure holds his horse by it's bridle; the middle figure holds a branding iron; and the bottom figure carries a coil of rope. The top figure of the agriculture sculpture hold his sack of cotton open as if to pour out the freshly picked bolls; the middle figure, an African American male, hefts a bale of cotton; and the bottom figure leads a mule by the bridle.

McVey was awarded the commission in 1941, but residents had to wait until 1948 for him to install the panels. The work had been set aside while the artist served in the Army Air Corps in the Pacific Theater.[201] When the sculptures did arrive in 1948, the people of Littlefield were baffled. Postmaster William D. T. Storey was "in the dark" about what the "two five-foot green panels" represented, but he was determined to find out. An article in the local newspaper revealed: "As far as he [the postmaster] could 'figure out,' one of the panels represents the Spanish regime in the Southwest, and the other the early cowboy days in this section. In fact one of the characters in the panel is holding an *LFD* branding iron in his hand."[202] The post office building was renovated and converted to county offices in 1997.

Livingston

"Buffalo Hunting" and "Landscape"

Theodore Van Soelen

Unavailable for viewing

"Buffalo Hunting"—4'6" × 12'; "Landscape"—7' × 34'

Oil on canvas

1940; 1941

$750; $1,000

Damaged when stripped from the walls of the former post office in 1997, in storage

A lapse in communication resulted in Livingston's receiving two murals for its post office. Artist Theodore Van Soelen adapted his first mural, "Buffalo Hunting," from his entry for the Amarillo competition. Other mural artists also commonly reused their mural designs. In the case of Livingston, however, the switch led to a public relations dilemma for the Section. The postmaster had asked for a "nice East Texas Painting." However, Van Soelen failed to contact him about his buffalo hunt idea. The artist insisted on painting buffalo, although buffalo were not part of the East Texas landscape. When the postmaster did not hear from the artist about the painting in progress, he wrote the Section, directly stating his preferences: "Our industry in this part of the State is oil, farming and saw milling. . . . I hope you can give us the painting [we want], and I assure you it will be appreciated."[203] When the artist still did not write him concerning the mural subject, the postmaster became suspicious and wrote curtly to Van Soelen: "You failed to state the picture you were painting, if it is not the proper painting for this part of East Texas, then we don't care for it."[204] Van Soelen did not respond. Believing the worst, the postmaster wrote an urgent message to the fourth assistant postmaster general, S. W. Purdum: "I will give you clearly the facts, and also the painting we expect, we are in the southern part of East Texas and cow boy [*sic*] or wild west painting is something we don't want. . . . We have the large pine tree forests, loblolly and long leaf (saw milling) oil, farming, cotton, corn, and all the vegetables, especially tomatoes, we shiped [*sic*] several cars from this

Co. last year."[205] Van Soelen, who by this time had already had made significant progress with his buffalo hunt painting, could no longer ignore the situation. He finally explained his position to Rowan. Enclosing the postmaster's letter, the artist noted that the letter "speaks for itself . . . and not in a soothing whisper either."[206] The artist explained apologetically that he overlooked responding to the postmaster because he thought that anything Washington had approved was automatically cleared: "I put my feelings away in moth-balls and wrote the postmaster a tactful letter as I did not want to bother you or stir up a fuss. It calmed his fears a little, I believe, but did no good so far as my mural is concerned. Evidently, they want a tomato packing scene. I do not have a prima-donna complex in such matters and up to now I have always had whole-hearted cooperation. How do you handle such situations?"[207]

Rowan, who had received a copy of the postmaster's letter to Purdum, already was moving to ward off further ill-feelings. In a letter to the postmaster, he indicated that he had read the postmaster's requests to the artist for the Livingston mural. However, he added, Van Soelen had already completed an Indian buffalo hunt scene, and the painting could not be unpainted; the contract could not be terminated. As a concession, Rowan informed the postmaster that he had found extra building funds and had commissioned Van Soelen to paint a second mural — this one to be more to the postmaster's liking. Van Soelen, of course, was both thrilled — to have another mural job — and relieved: "I am very pleased . . . . I had worked so long and hard on it ["Buffalo Hunting"] and I was discouraged because the people down there did not want a Western mural. Now I can go ahead and give them what they want to beautify the P.O., I hope."[208]

He then visited Livingston and met with citizens about their community. The second mural that he eventually created was more typical of East Texas. The painting covered the entire thirty-four-foot length of the post office lobby wall above the lock boxes. The mural consists of a Piney Woods landscape, with a cabin in the hazy distance, egrets along a pond, and a wild turkey on a stump. In addition, several oil wells and holding tanks in the background quietly indicate the integral influence of the oil industry on the Livingston economy. A moss-bearded live oak tree and cattle grazing in a meadow frame the right portion of the mural. A clock and three ventilation grills were removed from the wall after the painting had been installed, leaving unpainted rectangular spaces on the wall.

The experience of working with the people of Livingston gave Van Soelen's some important insights about Texans: "If they [Texans] do not like a thing they say so in a way you cannot misunderstand. Naturally, if they are convinced that you're first cousin of the tapeworm they are not going to like your specialty."[209] Fortunately, the people of Livingston wholeheartedly accepted the artist and his work.

Lockhart

"The Pony Express Station"

John Law Walker

Post Office

217 West Market Street

4′ × 10′

Oil on canvas

1939

$580

Good condition

For his mural at the Lockhart post office, John Walker combined the subjects of pioneers and of the U.S. Postal Service. His saga of settlement of this Texas Hill Country community features in the foreground a pony express rider speedily changing his tired horse for a fresh one, while an assistant dressed in buckskin holds the reins. The painting also presents a wagon train that begins in the distant hills. The line of settlers on wagons and on horseback curves its way through the picture to the central foreground. Indian figures with their horses dragging travois also find their way down from the ridge.

The people of Lockhart seemed to appreciate their mural, according to the postmaster at the time who wrote earnestly to Rowan: "I Wish to Say That The Mural Has Been Installed in The Lobby of This Post Office And is a Work of Art, Adding Quite a Lot to The Post Office Lobby. It Seems to Be All Right in Every Way And is Very Much Appreciated By The Writer And Our Patrons of This Office. It Is a Good Picture of Pioneer Days And Of Pony Express Days. I Thank You For Remembering This Historic Old Town With This Addition to Our Office."[210]

Longview

"Rural East Texas"

Thomas M. Stell, Jr.

Post Office

201 East Methvin Street

6′ × 15′11″

Oil on canvas

c. 1946

Good condition

In Thomas Stell's montage of East Texas agriculture, a farmer wearing a tall hat drives his flashy new tractor through the center of the farmyard. Symbols of prosperity clustered around him serve to remind mural viewers of America's potential: well-fed cows, a sturdy cabin, and a cartful of cotton pulled by two muscular horses alongside a railroad car.

During the depression, machines generally symbolized progress. Yet some people of rural Texas (see Farmersville entry), viewed machines with ambivalence and distrust, because they sometimes displaced workers.[211] Such apprehensive feelings did not seem common among the people of Longview, possibly because the mural was installed when the postwar economy began to boom.

Mart

"McLennan Looking for a Home"

José Aceves
Post Office
301 Texas Avenue
5′ × 12′
Oil on canvas
1939
$670
Excellent condition

In this mural by José Aceves, the towering figure of buckskin-clad Neil McLennan, for whom the county was named, embodies the spirit of the pioneer hero. Striking a proud and confident pose with his hand shadowing his forehead, McLennan searches the countryside around the Bosque River for a place to settle with his family. McLennan seems the epitome of courage. He holds a musket in one hand while beside him his son, who holds a stick in lieu of a musket, strikes a similar pose of confidence. McLennan's wife sits on the wagon in the background as she holds her child in her lap. From her position on the wagon, she regards her husband approvingly, while her daughter seated beside her looks out apprehensively over the prairie. In the background behind them, a trading post suggests the beginnings of settlement. The two powerful oxen in the foreground lean forward, almost out of the picture, to create dramatic visual depth in the painting.

Accuracy of historical detail took a back seat to political influence for the creation of one aspect of this mural. When Aceves did not include a landmark trading post in the background of his original design, U.S. Congressman W. R. Poage objected and insisted that the post be included. Poage stated as historical fact that McLennan had passed the post on his trek through what later became Bosque County. Aceves's research had turned up no such evidence. Rowan, however, asked the artist to compromise and include the post anyway, reasoning that "the charm or the intent of your composition would not be materially affected."[212] Aceves graciously acquiesced and proceeded to paint the trading post into the picture as a boon to local interests. Rowan was relieved to avoid a potentially damaging confrontation for the Section.

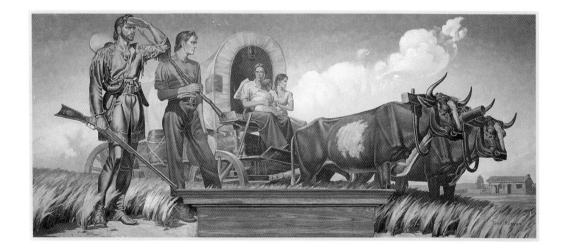

Mineola

"New and Old Methods of Transportation"

Bernard Zakheim

Unavailable for viewing

5'6" × 13'

Tempera on canvas

1938

$710

Destroyed[213]

Bernard Zakheim took advantage of people's fascination with symbols of movement—speeding trains, cars, and airplanes—in selecting a mural subject for Mineola. The town happened to be at the crossroads of two rail lines, a fact that generated considerable hope for economic progress in the small East Texas community.[214]

Zakheim's montage emphasizes the theme of progress. A set of railroad tracks runs through the center of the mural, separating the subject into two time frames. On the right, the artist included L. R. Graham, one of Mineola's first settlers, carrying an armful of supplies from the town's first general store, which Graham built in 1873. Graham and his African American helper, who carries a sack of

flour, are about to load supplies into a customer's horse-drawn buggy. However, the horse rears as if in reaction to the whistle of the approaching modern locomotive. Nearby, in the foreground, a mail carrier struggles to restrain his pack mule, which also rears in fright at the strange sound of the locomotive. The animals' rearing at the locomotive suggests the eclipse of the horse as a useful method of transportation. The left of the mural represents modern times. Two mail carriers dressed in uniform stand waiting on the loading platform with sacks of mail for the train's arrival. Bales of cotton also on the platform await loading. Meanwhile, overhead, an airplane sweeps across the cloudy horizon, symbolizing an even more advanced mode of mail transportation.

The mural had a positive effect on the artistic sensibilities of local folks. The postmaster keenly observed, "It seems that this mural has done quite a great deal for the people here, as there seems to be more interest in the beauty around us, and I believe the folks are getting art minded as you hear them calling each other's attention to the beautified sunset, beautiful clouds and just everything in general."[215]

An article in *The Mineola Monitor* praised Zakheim

and his work and indicated that the town was flattered to be the focus of attention. One Mineola citizen thanked the artist effusively for the mural, citing similar favorable responses from many other residents: "I have heard many citizens express their gratitude for the fine work in this picture and what it will mean to the coming generations to keep before them wonderful progress of time."[216] Visiting Mineola, the owner of a drug store in nearby Athens, Texas, saw Zakheim's mural and immediately wrote to the Section to request that his community's post office also be considered for receiving a mural.[217]

Mission

"Scenes along the Rio Grande"
Xavier Gonzalez
Unavailable for viewing
[Dimensions unknown]
Oil on canvas
1942
$950
Damaged in 1982 during removal from the old post office; rolled up in storage at the new post office[218]

The landscape in this mural represents the typical features of the region of the South Texas community of Mission. The mural's focus is a Texas Ranger standing on a bluff along the Rio Grande as he adjusts the saddle of his horse. The ranger's "watchful mood" comes after he hears gun shots from the Mexican side of the river.[219] Rangers in the early twentieth century guarded the border from Mexican revolutionaries who would raid ranches north of the river. Two prominent ranching symbols—a barbed-wire fence and the bleached longhorn skull—symbolize the ranching culture that dominated South Texas.

The local postmaster at first did not embrace news of a mural for his post office. The practical-minded official had a more prosaic idea for the use of government funds. In a letter to the assistant postmaster general, he expressed his thoughts directly: "If we have any choice, we prefer having an adding machine, as we need another one badly."[220] Despite the postmaster's mundane preferences, the artwork was completed and installed as planned. The people of Mission favored the mural, and Rowan congratulated the artist and remarked candidly: "The reaction of the general public to your work is most gratifying and, of course, those are the people for whom the work was intended, not the Postmaster alone. Fortunately, for the artists and for the program, we do not have to depend on the whims of petty officials."[221]

Odessa

"Stampede"

Tom Lea

Post Office

200 North Texas Street

5'6" × 16'9"

Oil on canvas

1940

$1,200

Restored

Tom Lea believed that the subject of a stampede was especially appropriate for Odessa's post office mural because of the city's proximity to the Horsehead Crossing of the Pecos River on the Goodnight-Loving cattle trail.[222]

Lea based his mural on a traditional cowboy ballad, "Little Joe the Wrangler." The mural captures a moment of wild rangeland drama when a cowboy is caught in a stampede of longhorns. Startled and terrified by a night-time electrical storm, the herd bolts in mad excitement. The frightened cattle's red eyes bulge. Caught in their path, the cowboy's horse, also terrified, hurls Joe headlong from the saddle. The mural freezes the action as Joe, suspended in mid-air, is about to tumble to his death in the ravine below. Some key lines from the ballad follow.

We was campin' on the Pecos when the wind began to blow
And we doubled up the guard to hold them tight
When the storm came roarin' from the north with thunder
*   and with rain*

And the herd stampeded off into the night!
Then amid the streaks of lightnin' we could see a horse
*   ahead,*
It was little Joe the Wrangler in the lead,
He was ridin' ol' Blue Rocket with a slicker o'er his head
And a-tryin' to check the cattle in their speed."[223]

The ballad ends tragically with Joe and his horse falling twenty feet down a "wash-out," and the hapless cowpoke is "mashed to a pulp" beneath his horse. Lea's vivid mural, of course, keeps the gruesome details of the tragedy implicit, satisfying the Section of Fine Arts' desire to keep negative images out of post office murals.

After abandoning its old post office in the 1970s, the U.S. Postal Service moved the mural to the new post office lobby located across the street. A vandal, however, put a gash in the mural canvas, which was mounted at eye level on one wall. The postal service and the community then had the canvas repaired and a guard rail installed in front of the painting to help protect it.[224]

"Stampede" remains a source of community pride. In 1993, city officials led a rededication ceremony for the mural. They presented Tom Lea, who was well into his eighties and was present as guest of honor, with an award of appreciation.

Quanah

"The Naming of Quanah"

Jerry Bywaters

Post Office

219 West Third Street

4′6″ × 14′

1938

Oil on canvas

$690

Good condition

Although the Panhandle was open early to cattlemen and buffalo hunters, others did not settle there until the coming of the railroads. In 1885, General G. M. Dodge, who named the town of Quanah, located on the outskirts of the panhandle, surveyed for the first railroad that ran through the county. In 1887, the first passenger train, the Fort Worth and Denver Railway, began service. Afterward, the town developed rapidly, basing its economy on cattle and hogs, cotton, wheat, and corn.

Jerry Bywaters's montage stresses the principal elements in this history and economic progress of what is now Hardeman County. Revered Comanche chief Quanah Parker, shown in full ceremonial attire faces a gun-toting white man. He holds a peace pipe prominently with one hand and with the other displays the sign of peace. Before Native Americans were displaced to Indian Territory, Quanah saw that the era of raids against whites was no longer

an option if his people were to survive. Bywaters's portrayal of Quanah as a peacemaker is based on the leader's wisdom to convince his followers to give up their raids and surrender to white control just at the time when a large contingent of U.S. troops was to be sent to end the conflicts. Thus, Quanah avoided certain defeat and the death of many people.

In the background of the mural Bywaters pictured a herd of buffalo roaming freely as they did in the days before commercial hunting destroyed them. Behind the buffalo herd, the artist included the prominent buttes that are located near Quanah. Settlers named these rock formations "Medicine Mounds," because the Comanche held them to be a sacred place for healing. Local residents, moreover, understood that Medicine Mounds is near the site where Texas Rangers recovered Cynthia Ann Parker, who as a child had been captured from white settlers and later became Chief Peta Nakoni's wife and the mother of the future chief Quanah Parker. In the mural's foreground a cowboy stands watch over a herd of cattle, a scene that represents the era of the cattle drives along the Pease River. The symbols of progress — mining, agriculture, ranching, manufacturing, oil, and the railroad — appear in the background to suggest the sequential development of those economic activities. As an additional tribute to progress, high-tension power lines run through the landscape, a reference to the building of the Lake Pauline dam by the West Texas Utility Company in the early 1900s.[225]

Ranger

"The Crossroads Town"

Emil Bisttram

Post Office

202 North Austin Street

4′6″ × 12′

Oil on canvas

1939

$880

Good condition

This mural portrays a peaceful scene in the early days of Ranger as imagined by artist Emil Bisttram. Farmers and ranchers stand to exchange news before the town's storefronts and the post office. The mural scene differs greatly from the scene the artist encountered when he visited Ranger in 1939. He found the shell of a former boom town, remnants of a once-prosperous community that had become full of the gaunt skeletons of empty brick buildings in a downtown that was in disrepair and partly aban-

doned. The bank had become home to an ice-cream store, and the old post office building had become a peanut storage space. The artist sadly assessed the situation for Rowan: "Before the oil boom of 1918 Ranger was the center of cotton production. This, of course, was shot to hell as soon as oil made it's [*sic*] appearance. Over night, like so many others, fortunes were made and since lost." A reminder of the town's former oil boom period was the "one lone refinery [that] continues to work spasmodically on a hillside . . . ."[226]

Although Bisttram considered the contemporary community of Ranger a pathetic sight, the artist had the vision to see the community as it once was and to link it with its future. He believed that the community still held greatness, and its hope lay in the resilience of its residents who were trying to make peanut farming the basis of the next boom. Bisttram acknowledged that the people's ability to endure and survive the vicissitudes of an economic roller coaster during periods of boom and bust demonstrated the town's real character.[227]

Robstown

"The Founding and Subsequent Development of Robstown"

Alice Reynolds

Post Office

313 Main Street

4′6″ × 13′5″

Oil on canvas

1941

$800

Good condition

Alice Reynolds's montage captures the bustle of activity surrounding a railroad land office when the South Texas community of Robstown was founded. Another vignette in the mural depicts a later time in the community's development when settlers frenetically prepare for an abundant harvest. Three wagons loaded with cotton make their way along the edge of the field toward the cotton gin in the background. In the extreme distance commercial structures of a prosperous little community symbolize the latest phase in the town's development. Reynolds described her original design as "full of interest and a good deal of conviction of the landscape."[228] Like most historical post office murals, town genesis murals such as this one provided people with a strong sense of continuity with the past. The idyllic images also seemed to present a challenge to the upcoming generation to carry the achievements of the community's past into the future.[229]

Rockdale

"Industry in Rockdale"

Maxwell Starr
Post Office
234 Ackerman Street
6′9″ × 16′
Oil on canvas
1947[230]
$700
Good condition

In the whirlwind of activity when the section was commissioning murals simultaneously across the country, officials sometimes reassigned mural jobs as a matter of convenience. Maxwell Starr originally planned a mural for the Baytown post office, but for bureaucratic reasons the Section changed the artwork's destination to Rockdale, a small community between Austin and Houston.[231]

Miners wielding pick and shovel dominate the center of interest of Rockdale's mural. Closely behind the miners the stark white bonnets and white dresses of four female field hands picking cotton create a distinctive visual contrast to the grimy mining activity. The prominent placement of the male cotton picker who struggles as he shoulders a large basket of cotton contributes movement to the bustle of field activity in the mural. In the background, various phases of the mining process take place as a large power shovel excavates the land and rail cars are being filled. In the central background, the artist placed a grove of pecan trees before rows of oil wells that are farther in the distance, indicating the area's unique agricultural and oil industries. Beyond, the field hand picking corn indicates another agricultural product, and in a clearing, to complete the idyllic image of Rockdale's busy prosperity, stand a farm house and windmill.

Today, low-hanging light fixtures partly obscure the mural and make viewing it awkward. Nevertheless, Maxwell Starr's striking montage creates an impressive drama of work and economic prosperity.

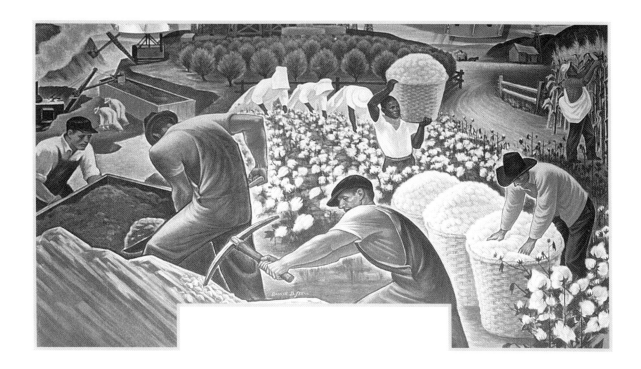

Rosenberg

"La Salle's Last Expedition"

William Dean Faucett

Unavailable for viewing

7′ × 12′

Tempera and oil on gesso board

1941

$850

Presumed destroyed[232]

Dean Faucett's mural projects the artist's vision of French explorer Robert Cavelier de La Salle as he is about to cross the Brazos River in East Texas and embark on an exploratory mission. A local history teacher had suggested that Faucett use La Salle as a subject.[233] As Faucett learned, La Salle had passed through the vicinity of present-day Navasota, Texas, about seventy miles to the north of Rosenberg, in about 1615. The French explorer had accidentally landed in Texas while seeking a sea approach to the mouth of the Mississippi River. Inaccurate maps and primitive navigation devices caused his three ships full of colonists and supplies to sail astray. As a result, La Salle overshot the Mississippi, landing on the Texas Gulf Coast.

Eventually, the explorer lost all his ships through mishap and was stranded in a hostile environment. The explorer established Fort St. Louis near present-day Port Lavaca and left behind a group of settlers while he and a small band of men attempted to reach French settlements on the Illinois River. La Salle's overzealous leadership style began to alienate his own men as they endured the obvious hardships of being stranded in the wilderness. They ultimately assassinated him.

Titled "La Salle's Last Expedition," Faucett's painting, however, focused on the positive aspects of La Salle's presence in the area without directly portraying the explorer's violent end. The artist tried to capture "all the feeling of the period and the sense of real importance that the exploration of the new world evoked at that time."[234] The mural depicts a young, energetic La Salle sitting mounted on his horse and eager to push on with his explorations. A boy holds the reins of the explorer's rearing horse as four members of his party regard them with ominous expressions. The sullen looks on the faces of some of La Salle's party seem to forebode their imminent misdeed. In the background a Catholic priest, the explorer's brother, sits on his horse ready to join the fateful journey.[235]

Rusk

"Agriculture and Industry"

Bernard Zakheim

Post Office

112 West Fifth Street

$3' \times 5'$

Tempera on Masonite

1939

$870

Fair condition, some flaking

Bernard Zakheim's montage for the Rusk post office depicts Cherokee County's economic mainstays: agriculture — producing peaches, tomatoes, and cotton — and the iron ore industry. The artist saw the mural as a fable of misuse of agricultural land and the heroic rescue of the federal government.[236] Zakheim's interpretation of regional history made the Indian figure to the left "indifferent to the peach industry which was developed by early white settlers who took the peach trees from the Cherokee Indians." The artist portrayed a dejected peach farmer sitting with rotting peaches at his feet, the result, according to the artist, of a lack of shipping facilities and modern, scientific knowledge of agriculture. Behind the farmer lies a badly eroded landscape, and, to the right, the ruins of an iron ore smelting plant. The distant ruins of Rusk College overlook the scene.[237] Zakheim represented the early Rusk settler T. G. Simpson practicing contour plowing on his field to prevent soil erosion. In 1895, neighbors mocked Simpson, according to Zakheim, for using conservation methods that the federal government would encouraged in the 1930s. In the foreground of the mural a Civilian Conservation Corps team engages in soil conservation and scientific farming activities. One of the CCC workers sprays tomatoes with insecticide; another examines the leaves for pests. "Through the help of the C.C.C. boys [the government] conserved the soil and made it possible for the farmer once more to live off his land," the artist explained.[238] As another plug for the federal government, Zakheim placed a mail carrier in the center of the pic-

ture. The federal government depended on mail service to bring farmers instructions for solving agricultural problems.

Despite Zakheim's inclusion of propaganda on behalf of the federal government, the Section of Fine Arts considered the mural esthetically inferior and did not immediately accept it. Over the course of several months, the Section followed Zakheim's progress closely, coaching him to improve the design as they saw fit. The Section administrators criticized the composition for not being very well organized and that Zakheim's figure drawing was an embarrassment. Referring to the figure of an agricultural worker who was portrayed spraying tomatoes, Rowan pointed out that the head was "unrelated" to the shoulders; he also called for "a more attractive type."[239] Rowan complained that the inclusion of the Indian did "not seem particularly significant to us." The Indian figure had round shoulders and a "strange face," Rowan wrote, and a "lack of relation between the fore part of the leg and the thigh," which "makes the figure look quite repellent."[240]

To justify its rigorous standards and his insistence on Zakheim's meeting them, Rowan tersely cited the Section's philosophic underpinnings. "Our attitude," he wrote to Zakheim, "is that, in addition to giving the public the message of art through a work of this kind, we want the work to be attractive enough to make them want to look at it again and again. I am being quite frank with you in stating that your work seems to hold very little such attraction."[241]

To appease the Section, Zakheim responded by sending Rowan a newspaper clipping that pictured the artist talking to a group of eager high school students backstage of the school auditorium where he worked on his mural cartoon. Although Zakheim offered this as evidence of his success at promoting good relations between citizens and the federal government, Rowan was not distracted from his purpose.

Months later, after making the suggested changes, Zakheim sent another photo of his revised work. Rowan still considered the cartoon unsatisfactory. He noted with seemingly brutal forthrightness that the landscape in general and the peach orchard in particular seemed unrealistic and a "toy-like affair which seems a contradiction to the realism of the figures."[242]

In frustration, the artist shared Rowan's letters with a sympathetic local businessman and supporter, Carey Williams of the Citizens State Bank. Williams promptly took up Zakheim's defense. Writing a caustic letter to Rowan, Williams called the criticisms "unfounded and ill-informed." He struck at the federal government's failures in social policy, trying to put Washington on the defensive, and called Rowan's pronouncement that the Indian in Zakheim's mural had no significance "ridiculous." He then went on to cite the importance of the Indians in the early history of the county, which was "named after one of the five civilized tribes [Cherokee] who were driven into this section by U.S. government troops out of the deep south and later driven out and into Oklahoma."

To Rowan's charge that the artist use a "more attractive type" of person to spray tomatoes, Williams pointed out what a public relations blunder it would have been if anyone in town had learned of it. "Your criticism would engender small friendship for you in this community if it be known, for in reality this figure is a rather accurate representation of a local athlete of a high type who is well liked

here." Williams concurred with one of Rowan's criticisms, however, and he relished telling the Washington administrator: "The information carried by the postman in the picture is stupid, but the fact remains that it is typical of what we obtain in our Post Office from the U.S. government." He pointed out that the three items depicted in Zakheim's mural still could be found hanging on the bulletin board of the local post office in the form of propaganda sent out by the Social Security board.

Williams then delivered the final blow of his attack, focusing on federal government art programs. After noting that numerous well-qualified individuals had favorably commented on Zakheim's cartoon, Williams wrote, "it would seem to me that the opinion of Mr. Thomas Craven, art critic and writer is justified. Says Mr. Craven: 'They don't want art, but just a lot of symbolic claptrap.'"[243]

Rowan kept his composure and did not budge from his position. In a response to Williams, he agreed on the importance of American Indians, but he specified that his problem with Zakheim's portrayal involved authenticity. He insisted that "the particular form used in the drawing of this figure was, in our estimation, not convincing to us nor would it be convincing to the general public."[244] Rowan then expressed his approval that Zakheim had used "local types" but added, after explaining the broader

purpose of the Section, that the artist would have to make the suggested changes anyway, on esthetic grounds.

Rowan's final justification to Williams was to frame the broad goal of Washington's agenda for art: "One cannot help but see that a truly indigenous American Art will be the result of the type of encouragement which you and the other citizens are giving to Mr. Zakheim. The attitude of this office is that we want the best possible decoration of which the artist is capable for the citizens of Rusk and you must bear with us in our efforts to produce that from Mr. Zakheim."[245] The artist eventually managed to meet the Section's standard of taste, and the mural finally was hung in 1939.

San Antonio

"San Antonio's Importance in Texas History"
Howard Cook
U.S. Post Office and Federal Courthouse
615 East Houston Street
6′ × 73′ (north and south walls)
6′ × 20′ (east and west walls)
Fresco
1939
$12,000
Excellent condition

Howard Cook's design of a six-foot-high continuous frieze running along the four walls above the arched portals in the foyer of the U.S. Post Office and Federal Courthouse in San Antonio won the national mural competition sponsored by the Section of Fine Arts.[246] Titled "San Antonio's Importance in Texas History," the mural represents a selection of significant historical events in San Antonio's history from the entrada along the Rio Grande of the first explorers—the Spanish conquistadors—to Texas' dramatic struggle to independence and its current history. The content of some of the panels and their symbolism, such as the battle of the Alamo and cattle drives, is obvious. However, many of the images leave today's observers guessing. Below is a summary modified from the artist's description of the mural contents, panel by panel.

South Wall: (1) Spanish conquistadors; Indian guide points to land of legendary wealth; priests and soldiers follow; conquistador holds Cabeza de Vaca's standard; overarch—mesa and mountains on border of the river. (2) Franciscan friars instruct Indians in agriculture and religion, while in the background, Indians labor to construct missions; overarch—Indian war dance contrasts to main scene. (3) In San Antonio Plaza, trade with Canary Island settlers, colonial days; background—solid-wheeled cart and Indians carrying heavy loads (left) suggest "Old Mexico"; sedan chair enters from right. (4) Mexico gains independence from Spain; townspeople welcome Mexican Republican soldiers as they cross the San Antonio River at Presidio of San Antonio; Mexican flag indicates Mexico's independent status. (5) Stephen F. Austin brings first pioneers who settled in South Texas; settlers (left) confront Indians; log house raising (right); background—view of the Gulf of Mexico in distance. (6) Death of Ben Milam (in arms of Samuel Maverick) after leading his men in capture of San Antonio; background—flag of Mexico and the red "no-quarter" flags flying over the Alamo.

West Wall: (7) Dramatic moment when Colonel William Travis draws a line in the dirt with his sword and asks for volunteers to stay at the Alamo and fight; Travis in center with Bowie and Crockett at right, and others. (8) Texas patriots make their heroic last stand against a wave of Mexican invaders inside the Alamo walls; overarch—battle flags of the Texas Revolution with slogans associated with the revolution.

North Wall: (9) Conclusion of Texas' struggle with Mexico; captured Mexican General Santa Anna stands before wounded Sam Houston, tended by a surgeon who bandages Houston's leg on the battlefield of San Jacinto;

"Deaf" Smith at Houston's side; overarch—Texas army camp, captains, and the Bayou. (10) First Congress of the Republic of Texas; Sam Houston presents his sword, symbolic of advancing from army commander to the first president of the Texas Republic; portraits of first cabinet members, including Stephen F. Austin, David G. Burnett, Lorenzo de Zavala, Mirabeau B. Lamar, Thomas J. Rusk, Juan Seguin, "Deaf" Smith, and William H. Wharton, all grouped before the Lone Star flag; overarch—ox-cart transportation. (11) Council House Fight;[247] Texans receive child hostage from Comanche chiefs, who are slipping their concealed weapons from under their blankets before their attack on Texans, symbolizing the beginning

of warfare with the Comanche; overarch—view of San Antonio, 1845. (12) Annexation, raising of U.S. flag in place of Lone Star; background—land rush, intensive colonization of land grants; overarch—Indians in buffalo hunt. (13) Importance of the cattle trail; cowboys driving herd of longhorns north to market. (14) Coming of industrial era to San Antonio; welcomers ushering in first railroad to San Antonio (Southern Pacific) with torch-light parade; Confederate flag indicates Texas' involvement in the Civil War.

East Wall: Developing the Natural Riches of Texas: (15) Agricultural pursuits of South Texas, signified by harvesting of rice and cotton. (16) Cattle ranch; modern cow-

boys in foreground; left center, vaqueros gathered around chuck wagon; herd of white-face cattle on range; over-arch — oil, a gusher's well being brought in.[248]

In a time when the stereotype of the artist as Bohemian commonly raised people's suspicions, Howard Cook passed the litmus test as a man of the people, an artist who knew how to paint and who was responsible and congenial to boot. He seemed to be generally appreciated and liked by local citizens.[249] Their view of the artist and their attitudes toward modern art are obvious from an article published in the San Antonio Rotary Club magazine. The article followed Cook's visit to the club as a guest speaker. It poked fun at modernism, the abstract European painting style widely emulated in the 1920s and '30s but generally not appreciated by nonacademic, working-class people. The article's author forcefully framed the sentiment about modernism: "In these days when the artists (so called) paint heads ten feet long on bodies two feet long and twist Mother Nature's nose until it aches, we've become a little timid about expressing our preference for real old-fashioned beauty that will still be beautiful many years from now and that knows no style or date." The article went on to welcome Cook to San Antonio and to praise him as "a really fine artist (in any man's language)."[250]

As an unofficial ambassador of the federal government, Cook seems to have made a good impression on at least some other San Antonio residents, as well. After the mural's completion, an article in the San Antonio Light praised Cook and his work even as it ridiculed artists in general: "At least we can say we have seen one artist who is modest, almost shy and not afraid to give out. Artist Cook we slip you one bunch of orchids. Your work fascinated us like a hypnotist does his victims. We can't go for these temperamental high hats but artist Cook was refreshing in his viewpoint."[251]

Nationally recognized as an accomplished muralist, Cook was master of the fresco, the technique of painting on wet plaster that was perfected in the Italian Renaissance and revived by a handful of Mexican painters in the

1920s. Some San Antonio residents who had never seen an artist at work were amazed to see Cook's frescoes slowly take shape on the walls of their new post office lobby. A constant stream of observers gathered in fascination or bewilderment to watch him work. Perched on his scaffold high above the foyer floor, Cook overheard the echoes and whispers of admirers, detractors, and the curious. The artist was so taken by some of the outspoken remarks that he kept a log of the most striking ones. For example, he noted the surprising exchange of two elderly ladies who tried to make sense of the scene of Santa Anna's surrender to Sam Houston after the Battle of San Jacinto. In the painting, a war-wounded Houston sits on a blanket, his back propped against a tree trunk. Before him stands the defeated Mexican General Santa Anna. At Houston's feet a surgeon kneels to bandage the general's wounded ankle. "What do you reckon they are doing in this one?" one lady asked. After a pause, her companion replied: "Looks to me like they're playing craps."[252]

On another occasion, as Cook stood on the lobby floor and studied the progress of his own work from below, a somber young man inquired who was painting the murals. Cook, perhaps anticipating a compliment, admitted responsibility, but the man replied boldly: "I don't know anything about art and in particular about this kind of painting — but they sure look like hell to me!"[253] On another occasion after he had stepped down from the scaffold, Cook recalled, "a cocky little man tapped me on the shoulder while I was apparently just a spectator on the Lobby floor and hissed confidently: 'That guy is getting 12,000 dollars for putting that stuff up there!'"

Cook, who used the faces of San Antonio residents for his model, finished the mural project in May, 1939, six months ahead of schedule.[254] The local postmaster reported that the completed project received many favorable comments from patrons and visitors. He testified on behalf of Cook: "I have seen murals at different points over the country, and without prejudice I think the job Mr. Cook did here ranks among the best."[255]

Seymour

"Comanches"

Tom Lea

Post Office

210 North Washington Street

5′ × 13′7″

Oil on canvas

1942

$950

Good condition

Many postmasters welcomed news that their station would receive a Section mural. However, when Seymour's postmaster learned that his post office was to receive a mural, he informed Washington: "Personally I would prefer the lobby without a mural, unless it depicts something of this section's history, and I think that is the general opinion of the citizenship."[256] Rowan enclosed a photo of Tom Lea's preliminary sketch of "Comanches" with his reply as proof that the subject definitely pertained to Seymour's history.[257] The mural portrays Comanches skillfully riding their horses bareback.

Lea, who also wrote novels of the southwest, detailed his rationale for his choice of subject matter. "The town [Seymour]," Lea wrote, "is in the heart of the former marches of the wild Comanches; and any old timer's eye will light up with a Comanche story at the mere mention of the name . . . . Among all the wild and daring and skillful riders North America has seen, authorities place the Comanches at the top of the list. So it is natural to paint them horseback — wild and free on the boundless plains in the early morning light."[258] The artist also lost no opportunity to expound on how Indians' spirit of freedom and individualism were as much a part of America's character as the spirit of the pioneers.

Smithville

"The Law—Texas Rangers"
Minette Teichmueller
Post Office
400 Main Street
5′ × 12′
Oil on canvas
1939
$670
Good condition

The mural for the Smithville post office depicts a mounted Texas Ranger apprehending two bandits who have paused beneath an old oak tree to divide loot they have just stolen. They raise their hands in surrender, looking down the bar-rel of the ranger's cocked revolver. An open money chest with cash scattered around it lies on the ground at their feet.

When Minette Teichmueller of San Antonio could find no other subject of local interest, she settled on the subject that would was sure to attract wide interest—the legendary Texas Rangers. As she reported flatly to Rowan: "There is practically no historical element to be considered [in the Smithville area], so I've made my design allegorical, and simple as the building calls for."[259] A Section of Fine Arts press release later quoted Teichmueller's words justifying her choice and cited her praise of the elite band of law enforcers. The artist asserted, "Texas Rangers are still known throughout the world for their cool courage and deadly aim."[260]

Teague

"Cattle Roundup"

Thomas M. Stell, Jr.

Post Office

320 Main Street

3′ × 8′

Oil on canvas

1940

$350

Good condition

In this mural, two cowboys drive longhorn cattle through a rugged West Texas landscape. At the base of the rock, an armadillo scurries between two saguaro cacti. An arroyo curves from right to left, vanishing into the distant hills toward a rock formation and clouds.

What is wrong with this picture? At first glance, nothing. However, consider that Teague is located in East Texas, and the details and landscape in the mural seem out of place. The treatment is quirky, almost satirical, or surrealistic. For example, the cowboy prominently wields what seems to be his bridle strap twisted into a brand-like shape, cleverly forming the artist's initials. Stell also intro-

duced some inauthentic elements. Behind the central figure, for example, a vulture sits hunched on the branch of a saguaro cactus — the latter being an obvious anomaly. Stell, who was born in Cuero, must have known that such a species of cactus does not grow in Texas. There is also something incongruous about the vulture's guarding her clutch of eggs on a rock below. It is unlikely that the vulture would have placed the eggs directly in the Texas sun, where they would quickly bake. The artist also playfully introduced an armadillo, a shy and reclusive creature of Texas folklore, but armadillos are not likely to be found in the open plains landscape that the painting portrays.

Such inauthentic details must have escaped Section administrators' scrutiny. The Section originally approved Stell's sketch with some modifications. Section officials principally suggested that Stell try to achieve greater realism by making "some penetrating observation" of the elements that he had chosen to include in the mural.[261] Section leaders deemed the horses and cattle too "toy like" and believed that the saddle and bridle were not authentic.[262] After Stell made the suggested changes to his mural, the Section accepted it, and it was installed.

Trinity

"Lumber Manufacturing"

Jerry Bywaters
Post Office
Main at Elm Streets
4'8½" × 16'
Oil on canvas
1942
$700
Good condition

Jerry Bywaters chose the operation of machinery at a lumber mill in East Texas as the subject of his mural for the Trinity post office. Visiting the Longleaf Pine Company, a large lumber plant in East Texas, the artist closely observed and was fascinated by the lumber manufacturing process and made numerous sketches of the most interesting parts.[263]

Bywaters was amazed to see how inside the typical lumber processing shed workers transformed pine logs into board lumber. He also found the teamwork of the mill workers inspiring. A Section of Fine Arts press release, which is based on Bywaters's description, clearly explains the process depicted in the mural: "After quickly studying each approaching log to see what kind of lumber it will best produce, the sawyer signals by hand to the setter — center man on the carriage — who sets the machinery controlling the width of the lumber to be cut. As the log is raised to the carriage, two men, called 'doggers,' at each end of the carriage clamp the log fast, and the log is then ready to be cut. After the first cutting, the rough lumber is then carried over endless conveyors to gang saws, edgers, trimmers and finally to the planing mill for dressing."[264]

Waco

"Cattle" and "Indians"

Eugenie Shonnard

Post Office

800 Franklin Avenue

Two panels—4′ × 6′ each

Relief sculpture in Texas gumwood

1939

$1,400

Good condition

Edward Rowan pronounced Eugenie Shonnard's Waco sculpture "wholly rife with an American spirit."[265] One of the panels, hung high on the lobby wall of Waco's ornate art deco post office, portrays a procession of Indians, including two females led by two male figures in full headdress. One of the women carries an infant; another carries a bowl of food on her head. A young child walks alongside them. In a border above the procession, the artist carved two beehive-shaped thatch dwellings, left and right ends, enclosing carvings of several live oak trees. In "Cattle," longhorns with gaunt, stylized features saunter along a trail. A border of live oak trees stretches across the top of the panel.

Waco residents were awed by and delighted with their post office murals. People's comments reflected popular perceptions of artists as a special kind of being. People seemed flattered and proud that this creator of culture had come to *their* town. An article in the *Waco Times Herald* announced gleefully that a "real artist" had arrived to install the murals. The reporter apparently was struck nearly speechless by the work, for he wrote: "No attempt will be made to give the briefest description of the skill displayed by Mrs. Shonnard or the artistic genius manifested in her creation; the panels must be seen to be appreciated. . . ."[266] The postmaster and Waco citizens praised the work. As the postmaster commented, "It is truly symbolic of the early days of Texas, the Indians and the steers, and many people view them and make favorable remarks daily."[267]

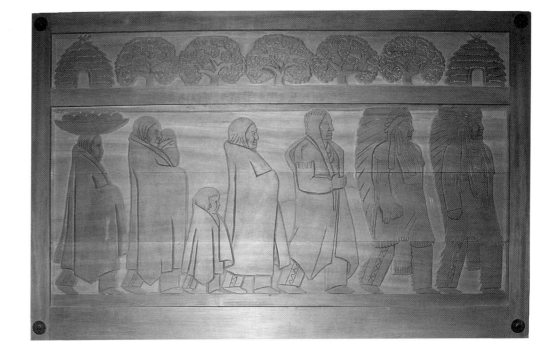

Wellington

"Settlers in Collingsworth County"

Bernard Arnest
Post Office
1000 West Avenue
5'6" × 13'
Tempera and oil on canvas
1940
$850
Good condition

This mural represents a group of settlers engaged in building a shelter and sowing crops on the plains of the Texas Panhandle — "fundamental activities of opening and using a new land," according to Bernard Arnest.[268] The artist intended to make the activities universal and not to designate any specific period or people. However, he consciously represented the Panhandle landscape and color.[269] His preliminary sketch delighted the Section of Fine Arts. Rowan commented on the "beautiful harmony of color in the design."[270] Of the completed mural, Rowan concluded: "There are some excellent passages of painting . . . and I congratulate you on your achievement."[271] Arnest's portrayal of the worker in the doorway wiping his brow particularly pleased Rowan, who marveled that the character still retained an attitude of wistfulness.[272]

GALLERY OF ADDITIONAL MURAL IMAGES

Amarillo, "Coronado's Exploration Party in Palo Duro Canyon" (detail) by Julius Woeltz (1941).

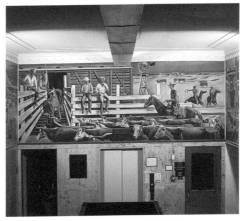

Amarillo, "Loading Cattle" by Julius Woeltz (1941).

Amarillo, "Gang Plow" by Julius Woeltz (1941).

Fort Worth, "Two Texas Rangers" by Frank Mechau (1940).

Houston, "Travis' Letter from the Alamo" by William McVey (1941).

Houston, "Houston Ship Canal—Early History: The Diana Docking" by Alexandre Hogue (1941).

Houston, "Houston Ship Canal: Loading Oil" by Jerry Bywaters (1941).

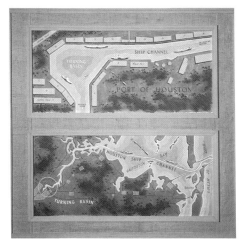

Houston, "Houston Ship Canal: Ship Turning Basin (Aerial View)" by Jerry Bywaters (1941).

Kilgore, "Contemporary Youth" by Xavier Gonzalez (1941).

Littlefield, "West Texas" by William McVey

Livingston, "Landscape" by Theodore Van Soelen (1941).

San Antonio, "Spanish Conquistadors" by Howard Cook (1939).

San Antonio, "Franciscan Friars Construct Mission" by Howard Cook (1939).

San Antonio, "Mexico's Independence" by Howard Cook (1939).

San Antonio, "Stephen Austin and Settlers" by Howard Cook (1939).

San Antonio, "Death of Ben Milam" by Howard Cook (1939).

San Antonio, "Death of Ben Milam" by Howard Cook (1939).

San Antonio, "Battle of the Alamo" by Howard Cook (1939).

San Antonio, "Council House Fight" by Howard Cook (1939).

San Antonio, "Torch-light Parade" by Howard Cook (1939).

San Antonio, "Cattle Ranch" by Howard Cook (1939).

Waco, "Cattle" by Eugenie Shonnard (1939).

LIST OF
TEXAS POST OFFICE MURALS

EXTANT POST OFFICE MURALS

	Location	Title	Artist	Date
1.	Alice (in storage)	"South Texas Panorama"	John Warren Hunter	1939
2.	Alpine	"View of Alpine"	José Moya del Pino	1940
3.	Alvin (in storage)	"Emigrants at Nightfall"	Loren Mozley	1942
4.	Amarillo	"Coronado's Exploration Party in Palo Duro Canyon"; "Gang Plow"; "Disk Harrow"; "Cattle Branding"; "Loading Cattle"; "Oil"	Julius Woeltz	1941
5.	Anson	"Cowboy Dance"	Jenne Magafan	1941
6.	Arlington (Arlington ISD Tax Office)	"Gathering Pecans"	Otis Dozier	1941
7.	Baytown (Baytown Historical Museum)	"Texas"	Barse Miller	1938
8.	Big Spring (Howard County Public Library)	"O Pioneers"	Peter Hurd	1938
9.	Borger (Hutchinson County Historical Museum)	"Big City News"	José Aceves	1939
10.	Brady	"Texas Immigrants"	Gordon K. Grant	1939
11.	Brownfield (Brownfield Police Department)	"Ranchers of the Panhandle Fighting Prairie Fire with Skinned Steer"	Frank Mechau	1940
12.	Bryan (Federal Building)	"Bison Hunt"	William Gordon Huff	1941
13.	Caldwell (Burleson County Courthouse)	"Indians Moving"	Suzanne Scheuer	1939
14.	Canyon	"Strays"	Francis S. Ankrom	1938
15.	Center	"Logging Scene"	Edward Chavez	1941

Location	Title	Artist	Date
16. Clifton	"Texas Longhorns — A Vanishing Breed"	Ila McAfee	1941
17. Cooper	"Before the Fencing of Delta County"	Lloyd Goff	1939
18. Corpus Christi (Nueces County Courthouse)	"The Sea: Port Activities and Harbor Fisheries"; "The Land: Agriculture, Mineral Resources, and Ranching"	Howard Cook	1941
19. Dallas (Federal Building)	"Pioneer Homebuilders"; "Airmail over Texas"	Peter Hurd	1940
20. Decatur	"Texas Plains"	Ray Strong	1939
21. Eastland	"Indian Buffalo Hunt"	Suzanne Scheuer	1938
22. El Campo	"Rural Texas Gulf Coast"	James Milford Zornes	1939
23. Electra	"Cattle"; "Oil"; "Wheat"	Allie Tennant	1940
24. Elgin	"Texas Farm"	Julius Woeltz	1940
25. El Paso	"Pass of the North"	Tom Lea	1938
26. Farmersville	"Soil Conservation in Collin County"	Jerry Bywaters	1941
27. Fort Worth (Federal Courthouse)	"Two Texas Rangers"; "The Taking of Sam Bass"; "Flags Over Texas"	Frank Mechau	1940
28. Fredericksburg	"Loading Cattle"	Otis Dozier	1942
29. Gatesville (New post office)	"Off to Northern Markets"	Joe De Yong	1939
30. Giddings	"Cowboys Receiving the Mail"	Otis Dozier	1939
31. Graham Young County Historical Museum)	"Oil Fields of Graham"	Alexandre Hogue	1939
32. Hamilton	"Texas Rangers in Camp"	Ward Lockwood	1942
33. Hereford	"On the Range"	Enid Bell	1941
34. Houston (Bob Casey Federal Building)	"Houston Ship Channel — Early History": "Construction of the Canal"; "The *Diana* Docking" "The Houston Ship Canal — Contemporary Scenes": "Loading Cotton"; "Loading Oil"; "Ship Turning Basin (Aerial View)"	Alexandre Hogue Jerry Bywaters	1941
35. Jasper (New post office)	"Industries of Jasper"	Alexander Levin	1939
36. Kenedy	"Grist for the Mill"	Charles Campbell	1939
37. Kilgore	"Drilling for Oil"; "Pioneer Saga"; "Music of the Plains"; "Contemporary Youth"	Xavier Gonzalez	1941
38. La Grange	"Horses"	Tom E. Lewis	1939
39. Lamesa	"The Horse Breakers"	Fletcher Martin	1939
40. Lampasas	"Afternoon on a Texas Ranch"	Ethel Edwards	1941
41. Liberty (New post office)	"The Story of the Big Fish"	Howard Fisher	1939
42. Linden	"Cotton Pickers"	Victor Arnautoff	1939
43. Littlefield	"West Texas"	William McVey	1948
44. Livingston (in storage)	"Buffalo Hunting"; "Landscape"	Theodore Van Soelen	1940; 1941

Location	Title	Artist	Date
45. Lockhart	"The Pony Express Station"	John Law Walker	1939
46. Longview	"Rural East Texas"	Thomas M. Stell, Jr.	c. 1946
47. Mart	"McLennan Looking for a Home"	José Aceves	1939
48. Mission (in storage)	"Scenes along the Rio Grande"	Xavier Gonzales	1942
49. Odessa	"Stampede"	Tom Lea	1940
50. Quanah	"The Naming of Quanah"	Jerry Bywaters	1938
51. Ranger	"The Crossroads Town"	Emil Bisttram	1939
52. Robstown	"The Founding and Subsequent Development of Robstown"	Alice Reynolds	1941
53. Rockdale	"Industry in Rockdale"	Maxwell Starr	1943
54. Rusk	"Agriculture and Industry"	Bernard Zakheim	1939
55. San Antonio	"San Antonio's Importance in Texas History"	Howard Cook	1939
56. Seymour	"Comanches"	Tom Lea	1942
57. Smithville	"The Law — Texas Rangers"	Minette Teichmueller	1939
58. Teague	"Cattle Roundup"	Thomas M. Stell, Jr.	1940
59. Trinity	"Lumber Manufacturing"	Jerry Bywaters	1942
60. Waco	"Cattle"; "Indians"	Eugenie Shonnard	1939
61. Wellington	"Settlers in Collingsworth County"	Bernard Arnest	1940

DESTROYED OR LOST POST OFFICE MURALS

Location	Title	Artist	Date
62. College Station	"Good Technique — Good Harvest"	Victor M. Arnautoff	1938
63. Conroe	"Early Texans"	Nicholas Lyon	1938
64. Edinburg	"Harvest of the Rio Grande"	Ward Lockwood	1940
65. Henderson	"Local Industries"	Paul Ninas	1937
66. Houston	"Travis' Letter from the Alamo"; "Sam Houston's Report on the Battle of San Jacinto"	William McVey	1941
67. Kaufman	"Driving the Steers"	Margaret A. Dobson	1939
68. Mineola	"New and Old Methods of Transportation"	Bernard Zakheim	1938
69. Rosenberg	"La Salle's Last Expedition"	William Dean Faucett	1941

TEXAS POST OFFICE MURALS
ARRANGED BY SUBJECT

FOLKLORE/LEGEND
Anson
Clifton
Eastland
Fort Worth
Hamilton
Liberty
Odessa
Smithville

HISTORY: EARLY SETTLEMENT/PIONEERS
Alvin
Big Spring
Borger
Brady
Conroe
Cooper
Dallas
El Paso
Kilgore
Mart

Ranger
Wellington

HISTORY: SPECIFIC EVENTS
Amarillo
Houston
Rosenberg
San Antonio

INDIANS
Amarillo
Bryan
Caldwell
Eastland
Livingston
Seymour
Waco

PROGRESS
Alpine
Arlington
Baytown

College Station
Farmersville
Mineola
Rusk

TOWN FOUNDING
Mart
Quanah
Robstown

U.S.MAIL
Alpine
Baytown
Borger
Dallas
Giddings
Lockhart
Ranger

WORK/INDUSTRY
Amarillo
Arlington

113

Brownfield	Fredericksburg	Kenedy
Canyon	Gatesville	Lamesa
Center	Graham	Linden
Cooper	Henderson	Littlefield
Corpus Christi	Hereford	Longview
Edinburg	Houston	Rockdale
Electra	Jasper	Teague
Elgin	Kaufman	Trinity

TEXAS POST OFFICE
MURAL ARTISTS

JOSÉ ACEVES (b. 1909, El Paso–d. 1968, El Paso) was a naturalized American citizen. Born in Chihuahua, Mexico, in 1909, his family immigrated to El Paso during the Mexican Revolution. Aceves studied art informally with his friends Audley Dean Nichols and Tom Lea; the latter recommended him to the Section of Fine Arts. In addition to the Section murals he completed for the Borger and Mart, Texas, post offices, he painted murals for the Paso del Norte Hotel in El Paso and the Banco Commercial in Chihuahua, Mexico. Aceves served three years in the U.S. Navy during World War II then worked as an illustrator in San Diego, California. His formal art training included attendance at the American Academy of Art in Chicago and classes at the Dallas Museum of Art (formerly Dallas Museum of Fine Arts). His work was exhibited at the 1936 Texas Centennial, the El Paso Centennial, and the Dallas Museum of Art.[1]

FRANCIS S. ANKROM (b. 1862, Allenville, Ohio–d. 1952, San Antonio, Texas) studied at Ohio Northern University then at Garret Bible Institute, in Evanston, Illinois, after attending public schools. For a time he also studied law in Chicago. After serving in the U.S. Army during World War I, he made his home in San Antonio and practiced architecture. Ankrom had painted murals as a hobby for fifteen years when he received the commission to paint the Canyon, Texas, post office mural. He was affiliated with the San Antonio Art League and the Texas Fine Arts Association.[2]

VICTOR M. ARNAUTOFF (b. 1896, Mariupol, Ukraine, Russia — d. 1979, Leningrad, Russia) studied at the California School of Fine Art in San Francisco with Ralph Stackpole, Edgar Walters, and Diego Rivera. He arrived in San Francisco in 1925 after stays in China and Mexico. He returned to China after completing his studies, then, with his wife and children, he emigrated to Mexico. In 1931, he moved back to San Francisco. When his wife died, he returned to Russia. Arnautoff was an educator and graphic artist as well as a painter. He was an instructor in sculpture and fresco painting at the California School of Fine Art and assistant professor in the art and architecture department of Stanford University. His public murals include work on the PWAP-sponsored murals in Coit Tower, San Francisco, and the post offices in Linden and College Station, Texas, as well as those in Richmond and Pacific Grove, California.[3]

BERNARD P. ARNEST (b. 1917, Denver, Colorado — d. 1986) studied at the Colorado Springs Fine Arts Center with Boardman Robinson. A 1940 Guggenheim Fellow, he later served as a U.S. Army war artist beginning in 1942, and then as chief war artist for the European Theater Headquarters 1944–45. He had a long and successful career as an artist and teacher, including positions at the Minneapolis School of Art, the University of Minnesota, and Colorado College, where he was chairman of the art department from 1957 to 1971. His work has been exhibited at shows regionally and nationally.[4]

ENID D. BELL (b. 1904, London, England) studied at the Glasgow School of Art in Scotland, with Sir W. Reid Dick in London, at the John's Wood School of Art in London, and with the Art Students League of New York. Bell lived in North Bergen and Englewood, New Jersey. She exhibited widely and won numerous prizes in the 1930s and 1940s in New Jersey and Santa Fe, New Mexico. She completed mural relief sculptures for post offices in Mt. Holly, New Jersey, and Hereford, Texas. She held the position of sculpture supervisor 1940–41 for the Federal Art Project for New Jersey, and she was instructor of sculpture and head of the department of the Newark School of Fine and Industrial Art, 1944–68. She resigned this position when she moved to Englewood, New Jersey, with her husband, a painter. Bell gave private art lessons and taught art at the Saturday School for Gifted Children in Oradell, New Jersey. She also published articles in *American Artist* magazine, lectured, and demonstrated sculpture techniques. She completed five relief sculptures for the American Cultural Foundation in Cambridge, Massachusetts, and a bronze relief panel for the Beth Israel Hospital in Newark, New Jersey.[5]

EMIL JAMES BISTTRAM (b. 1895, Hungary–d. 1976, Taos, New Mexico) emigrated to the United States at age eleven. He studied art at the New York School of Fine and Applied Arts, the National Academy, and the Cooper Union. He taught at the New York School of Fine and Applied Arts and the Master Institute of the Roerich Museum. In 1931, upon being awarded the Guggenheim Fellowship, he worked with Diego Rivera. He went on to found in 1932 the Taos School of Art, which became known as the Bisttram School of Fine Arts, later established in Phoenix and Los Angeles.[6]

JERRY BYWATERS (b. 1906, Paris, Texas–d. 1989, Dallas): Bywaters received his bachelor of arts degree from Southern Methodist University in Dallas. He continued his studies at the Dallas Art Institute under Olin Travis and Thomas Stell. He also studied briefly at the Art Students League of New York, as well as on field trips to Europe. He visited Mexico and met Diego Rivera and other muralists, then wrote about them. An art critic for the *Dallas Morning News* from the 1930s and a longtime contributor to the *Southwest Review*, Bywaters was a spokesman for regionalist art. He was a founding member of Lone Star Printmakers and a member of the Dallas Nine circle of artists. A professor of art at SMU, he also served as chairman of the division of fine arts from 1965 to 1967. From 1943 to 1964 he served as director of the Dallas Museum of Fine Art and then became head of the Pollock Gallery at SMU until 1970. As an active educator and critic, his art was recognized nationally. His works, which appear in numerous museums and private collections, feature the Texas landscape, as well as still lifes and portraits. In addition to murals in the Farmersville, Houston, Quanah, and Trinity post offices, he painted a mural for the Carnegie Library in Paris, Texas, and, under the Public Works of Art Project, a series of nine murals (now destroyed) with Alexandre Hogue for the Dallas City Hall.[7]

CHARLES CAMPBELL (b. 1905, Dayton, Ohio–d. 1985, Phoenix, Arizona) studied at the Cleveland School of Art and exhibited in the Museum of Modern Art, Washington, D.C., in 1938. In addition to completing the mural for the Kenedy, Texas, post office, he also painted the mural for the U.S. post office in Angola, Indiana, and was employed in WPA art projects.[8]

EDWARD A. CHAVEZ (b. 1917, Wagonmound, New Mexico; d. 1995) studied at the Colorado Springs Fine Arts Center and with Boardman Robinson and Frank Mechau. A painter, sculptor, and lithographer, Chavez's awards included a Tiffany Foundation grant and a Fulbright scholarship to study in Italy. His murals include those in West

High School in Denver, Colorado, and the U.S. Post Offices in Center, Texas, and Glenwood Springs, Colorado. He held teaching positions at the Art Students League of New York (1954–58) and the Syracuse University School of Art (1960–62).[9]

HOWARD COOK (b. Springfield, Massachusetts–d. 1980) was living and working in Ranchos de Taos, New Mexico, when he received the commission for the federal courthouse and post office in San Antonio. He studied at the Art Students League of New York and traveled in Europe, Turkey, the Far East, North Africa, and Central America. In 1932, a Guggenheim fellowship allowed him to work and travel for a year in Mexico and a year in the Southwest United States. He completed two frescoes in the Springfield, Massachusetts, courthouse under the Public Works of Art Project before painting the mural sequence for the federal courthouse and post office in San Antonio. He also painted the murals at the Corpus Christi post office and one for the post office of Tasco, New Mexico, where he lived for a time. Cook also lived in San Antonio, Corpus Christi, and Southeast Texas, where he recorded aspects of rural and agricultural life. He received the gold medal of honor awarded by the Architectural League of New York City for his fresco in one of the courtrooms of the Pittsburgh, Pennsylvania, Post Office and Courthouse, which was the result of a national competition by the Section of Fine Arts. Cook taught art at the University of Texas at Austin, the University of New Mexico, Albuquerque, and the University of California at Berkeley, among other institutions. He served as an artist correspondent in the South Pacific during World War II.[10]

JOSÉ MOYA DEL PINO (b. 1891, Córdoba province, Spain–d. 1969) began his art career atypically. At age ten he was apprenticed to a traveling artist who painted religious pictures and patron saints and sold them to peasants and small village churches. At sixteen, he began studies at the Academy of Fine Arts in Madrid, from which he graduated with honors. He associated with Spanish Post-Impressionists Juan Gris and Diego Rivera, among others. After del Pino painted the portrait of King Alfonso III of Spain in the early 1920s, the king asked him to accompany a traveling exhibit of Diego Rodrigo de Silva Velásquez's artwork. The exhibit took del Pino to San Francisco, where he settled and began earning a living as a portrait artist. In 1934, he painted a mural for the Public Works of Art Project at Coit Tower in San Francisco. His other public murals are located at Redwood City and San Rafael, California, as well as the mural for the post office in Alpine, Texas. Del Pino won many awards during his career.[11]

JOSEPH "JOE" F. DE YONG (b. 1894, Webster Grove, Missouri–d. 1975, Los Angeles), a painter and sculptor, was a deaf cowboy artist who became associated with the movie industry in Los Angeles, where he played small parts in Tom Mix movies. Taking an interest in American Indian culture, he learned Indian sign language and became technical adviser on Indians for various movies. He completed works for the Santa Barbara Free Public Library, the Cowboy Hall of Fame in Oklahoma City, as well as the mural for the Gatesville, Texas, post office.[12]

MARGARET A. DOBSON (b. 1888, Baltimore, Maryland–d. 1981, Los Angeles, California) studied at the Maryland Institute, Syracuse University, and the Fontainebleau School of Fine Arts. A painter, craftsperson, writer, and lecturer, Dobson moved to California and in 1938 exhibited at the California Pacific International Exposition. Her work won several awards, including a 1927 Fontainebleau prize and a 1930 medal from the City of Paris, France. In addition to her mural for the Section of Fine Arts at the Kaufman, Texas, post office, she painted murals for the Girl Scout Building in Santa Monica, California, and the U.S. Navy.[13]

OTIS DOZIER (b. 1904, Forney, Texas–d. 1987, Dallas), a native of Lawson, Texas, spent his youth in nearby Forney on a cotton farm. In 1921, his family moved to Dallas where he took art lessons from Vivian Anspaugh and later with

Frank Reaugh. In 1937, he received a scholarship to study at the Fine Arts Center in Colorado Springs, where he later joined the faculty along with Boardman Robinson. He remained on the faculty until 1945. A Dallas regionalist, he was also considered an important member of the Lone Star Printmakers group in the 1940s. His work has won many awards nationally. His Section of Fine Arts work includes murals for the post offices in Arlington, Giddings, and Fredericksburg, Texas. Other murals by Dozier are located in the Texas A&M University Library, College Station; Forest Avenue High School, Dallas; and the First National Bank of Mesquite.[14]

ETHEL EDWARDS (*b. 1914–d. 1999*) attended Sophie Newcomb College School of Art in New Orleans, where she studied under Xavier Gonzalez, and at Tulane University. Edwards and Gonzalez married in 1935. Her work was represented at a 1939 show of contemporary American women painters in Wichita, Kansas, and a one-person show the same year at the Newcomb College Arts and Crafts Club state exhibition in Shreveport, Louisiana. She and Gonzalez moved to New York City, and each kept a separate studio. They spent summers in Wellsfleet, Massachusetts, where they operated a painting school. She also taught at the Art Students League of New York.[15]

WILLIAM DEAN FAUCETT (*b. 1913, Price, Utah–d. 1998*) studied at Brigham Young University, the Art Students League of New York, National Institute of Architectural Education, and the Colorado Springs Fine Arts Center. He also studied with Boardman Robinson and others. Throughout his career, Faucett exhibited widely, including shows at the Witte Memorial Museum in San Antonio and the Corcoran Gallery in Washington, D.C. His works won numerous prizes, among them his submissions to shows at the Carnegie Institute (1942) and the Salmagundi Club (1946). He was a Guggenheim fellow 1943–45. His Section of Fine Arts murals include those for the U.S. post offices at Augusta, Georgia; West New York, New Jersey;

and Rosenburg, Texas. He also painted murals for Grant's Tomb in New York and for Randolph Field in San Antonio. Sites of his other public works include the U.S. Air Force Academy in Colorado Springs and the U.S. Air Force Armed Forces Committee Room at the U.S. Capitol. He has lived in Dorset, Vermont, and New York City.[16]

HOWARD FISHER (*b. and d. unknown*) lived in San Antonio and later moved to Wimberley, an artists' community north of New Braunfels.

LLOYD LOZES GOFF (*b. 1917, Dallas–d. 1982, New York City*) studied with Frank Reaugh and Frank Klepper, as well as with Thomas Stell and Olin Travis at the Dallas Art Institute. In 1932, he exhibited his work at the Nine Young Dallas Artists show in Dallas. He exhibited widely in Texas, New York, and Mexico. His murals include a 1938 work with Paul Cadmus for the U.S. Embassy in Ottawa, Canada; frescoes with Reginald Marsh at the Customs House in New York City; and Section of Fine Arts post office murals for Cooper, Texas, and Hollis, Oklahoma. He painted other murals for the New York City Municipal Building and Southern Methodist University, Dallas. He studied 1940–42 at the University of New Mexico, Albuquerque, and later held teaching positions there for several years. He illustrated several books, including one he authored, *Fly Redwing Fly* (New York: Lothrop, Lee & Shepherd Co., 1959).[17]

XAVIER GONZALEZ (*b. 1898, Almeria, Spain–d. 1999, New York City*) and his family moved to Puebla, Mexico, early in his life. In Mexico City, he studied at the San Carlos Academy. He also studied mechanics by correspondence and worked as a draftsman at a railroad company. After World War I, he immigrated to the United States and worked for a railroad company in Iowa and as a window dresser in Chicago, where he studied at the Art Institute of Chicago in the evenings. In 1925, he moved to San Antonio and taught at the Witte Memorial Museum. He became a U.S. citizen in 1930. From 1933 to 1939 he was director of the Summer School of Art at Sul Ross State Teachers College in Alpine, Texas. He held teaching positions at Sophie Newcomb College and Tulane University. Two of his students — Ethel Edwards, whom he married in 1942, and Suzanne Scheuer — painted post office murals in Texas. After moving to New York City, Gonzalez also taught at the Brooklyn Museum Art School. He won numerous awards, including a 1947 Guggenheim Fellowship and a 1965 Ford Foundation grant.[18]

GORDON K. GRANT (*b. 1875, San Francisco–d. 1962, New York City*) became renowned as a marine painter. His works have appeared widely in magazines and have been published as prints. He covered the Boer War in South Africa for *Harper's* and was an illustrator for *Puck*, 1901–1909. A prolific artist, his works were exhibited in such places as the Kendall Whaling Museum, the Mystic Seaport Museum, the U.S. Naval Academy, the White House, and the Corcoran Gallery. His post office murals appear in Kennebunkport, Maine, and Brady, Texas. He later gained wide recognition as an author/illustrator of *Ships Under Sail* (1941), *The Secret Voyage* (1943), and several stories.[19]

ALEXANDRE HOGUE (*b. 1898, Memphis, Missouri–d. 1994, Tulsa, Oklahoma*) moved as an infant to Denton, Texas, and then to a ranch near Dalhart, where he was raised. He studied at the Minneapolis College of Art and Design, returning to Dallas as an illustrator for the *Dallas Morning News*. In 1921, he relocated to New York City and held positions as a designer with advertising firms. On summer visits to Texas, he frequently accompanied Frank Reaugh on sketching outings. He returned to Dallas in 1925 to paint full time. He taught summer classes at the Texas State College for Women from 1931 to 1942. From 1936 to 1942 he headed the art department at the Hockaday School for Girls. During World War II he worked as an illustrator for the North American Aviation Corporation in Grand Prairie. Later, he joined the faculty of the University of Tulsa, where he was subsequently named head of the art department. Hogue was a member of the Lone Star Printmakers and the Dallas Nine circle of artists that included Jerry Bywaters, Harry P. Carnohan, John Douglass, Otis Dozier, William Lester, Perry Nichols, Everett Spruce, and Thomas M. Stell, Jr. Hogue is known for his southwestern landscapes that emphasize destruction of the land through mismanagement. In 1937, *Life* magazine featured his series on the Dust Bowl. His work has been exhibited extensively in this country and in Europe.[20]

WILLIAM GORDON HUFF (*b. 1903, Fresno, California*) studied at the California College of Fine Art and the California School of Arts and Crafts, as well as the Beaux-Arts Institute in New York City and the Ecole de la Grande Chaumiere in Paris. His sculpture won numerous prizes, including first prize in the 1923 San Francisco Art Academy show. His works include the Civil War Monument at Bennington, Vermont, and various other monuments in New England and California.[21]

JOHN WARREN HUNTER (*b. 1904, London, [Kimble County,] Texas–d. 1993, San Antonio*) was raised in San Antonio. He worked as a printer with his father, who was a newspaper publisher of several weekly newspapers in Arizona. Hunter attended the Art Institute of Chicago in 1939, graduating with honors. He then returned to San Antonio and soon received a commission to paint the post office mural at Alice, Texas. He had a long career as a commercial artist and art teacher. He taught art classes at the Witte Memorial Museum School of Art in San Antonio. During World War II he worked for the U.S. Army Map Services. After the war, he resumed teaching classes at the Witte until 1952. He taught art 1946–61 at his Hunter School of Art in La Villita (downtown San Antonio). He also taught at the San Antonio Art Institute from 1946, becoming the school's dean in 1951. As a commercial artist, he contributed to *Ford Times* magazine and illustrated history textbooks.[22]

PETER HURD (b. 1904, Roswell, New Mexico–d. 1984, Roswell, New Mexico) studied at the Pennsylvania Academy of Fine Arts and with N. C. Wyeth. He exhibited widely, winning a prize at a 1937 Art Institute of Chicago show. His work also won prizes from the Wilmington Society of Fine Arts in 1930, 1941, and 1945, as well as numerous other awards throughout his career. He was a war correspondent 1942–45 for *Life* magazine and was awarded the European Theater Medal for service overseas. In addition to painting Section of Fine Arts murals for post offices in Big Spring and Dallas, Hurd completed murals for the Prudential Insurance Company in Houston and a sixteen-panel fresco for the rotunda of the West Texas Museum on the campus of Texas Tech College in Lubbock (1957). President Dwight Eisenhower appointed him to the National Commission of Fine Arts in 1959. In 1966, the White House Historical Association commissioned him to paint the official portrait of President Lyndon B. Johnson. A painter of the Southwest landscape and subjects, Hurd has been placed among other important American Scene artists, including Thomas Hart Benton, John Steuart Curry, Leon Krol, Reginald Marsh, Grant Wood, and Andrew Wyeth.[23]

TOM LEA (b. 1907, El Paso, Texas–d. 1999, El Paso) studied at the Art Institute of Chicago 1924–26. He studied mural painting with muralist John W. Norton in Chicago and worked as Norton's studio assistant. In 1930, he traveled and studied in Italy. His work was included in *Life* magazine's "48 States Competition" (1939) of post office murals. In 1936 he was one of several artists to be chosen to decorate the State of Texas Building for the Texas Centennial at Fair Park in Dallas. He painted murals for private residences in Chicago, El Paso, and Santa Fe. He has won many awards and prizes, including a 1940 prize from the Museum of Fine Arts, Houston. Public murals include the South Park Commission building in Chicago, and Public Works of Art Project murals for College Library in Mosilla Park, New Mexico. His murals also appear in the Las Cruces, New Mexico, Public Library. His mural, "The Nesters," was commissioned in the 1930s for the new Post Office Department Building in Washington, D.C. In addition to painting Texas post office murals, Lea painted a mural for the post office in Pleasant Hill, Missouri. Lea illustrated for the *Saturday Evening Post* magazine in 1939 and books by J. Frank Dobie, including *Apache Gold and Yaqui Silver* (Little, Brown, 1939), *The Longhorns* (1940), and others. During World War II he was a war correspondent for *Life* magazine, painting numerous combat scenes in Europe and the East.[24]

ALEXANDER LEVIN (b. 1907, Russia–unknown) emigrated to the United States in 1923 and later became a U.S. citizen. He studied at the Oakland School of Arts for a year, then entered the Pennsylvania Academy of Fine Arts in Philadelphia. He traveled in Europe on a scholarship to study the masters and developed an appreciation for the relation of architecture to mural painting. Returning to the United States, he studied architecture at the University of Southern California, Los Angeles, and received his bachelor's degree in 1935. He taught art at the Hesse Art Gallery in Glendale for a year and later worked in the Los Angeles office of architect Paul R. Williams. He exhibited in the Pennsylvania Academy of Fine Arts, Philadelphia, and was awarded first prize in still life painting at a 1931 show sponsored by the Society of Washington Artists. In 1938, at the time of his Jasper, Texas, mural commission, he also was painting a mural for owners of a private residence in California. Levin's work is represented in numerous private art collections.[25]

TOM E. LEWIS (b. 1909, Los Angeles–d. 1979, San Francisco) studied architecture at the University of Southern California. A self-taught artist, Lewis exhibited his work in Southern California and at the Corcoran Gallery three times between 1935 and 1941. He completed post office murals at Hayward and Placerville, California, as well as La Grange, Texas.[26]

WARD LOCKWOOD (b. 1884, Atchison, Kansas–d. 1963, Talpa, New Mexico) studied at the University of Kansas, University of Pennsylvania Academy of Fine Arts (1914–16), and the Academy Ransom, Paris. He served in World War I, rising to the rank of captain. He was a commercial artist 1922–24 in Kansas City, Missouri, then he moved to Taos, New Mexico, where he taught art at the Taos Field School of Art. In 1932, he began the lithography program at the Colorado Springs Fine Arts Center. He also taught for a year at the University of New Mexico, Albuquerque, before taking a position at the University of Texas at Austin, where he organized the art department. He then served in World War II as colonel at the Aviation Cadet Center, U.S. Army Air Corps, in San Antonio. After the war, he resumed his position as professor at the University of Texas. In 1948, he was appointed a member of the faculty at the University of California at Berkeley, where he stayed until 1961, retiring thereafter to New Mexico. He illustrated the book *Adventures of a Texas Naturalist* by folklorist Roy Bedicek (Austin: University of Texas Press, 1961). Lockwood painted murals for the Post Office Department Building in Washington, D.C., the Federal Courthouse in Lexington, Kentucky, and post offices in Edinburg, Texas, and Wichita, Kansas, among those in other public buildings in various locations.[27]

NICOLAS LYON (b. 1900, Flatonia, Texas—unknown) studied at the University of Texas and continued at the University of Houston, where he took architecture courses. His main interest, however, shifted to art, and he pursued his art studies at the Yale School of Fine Arts under Eugene Savage. Lyon painted portraits of several former chief justices of the Supreme Court of Texas. In addition to his mural for the Conroe, Texas, post office (destroyed), he painted one at Albert Sidney Johnson High School in Houston.[28]

ILA MCAFEE (b. 1900, Gunnison, Colorado–d. 1995) attended Western State College, Gunnison, Colorado, then studied at the Art Students League of New York and the National Academy of Design, also in New York City. She and her husband, a painter, Elmer Turner, settled in Taos, New Mexico. Her U.S. post office murals include those at Cordel and Edmond, Oklahoma; Gunnison, Colorado; and Clifton, Texas. She also painted murals for the public library of Greeley, Colorado, and for Amarillo [Texas] High School and Baylor University, Waco, Texas. McAfee was an illustrator of children's books, and she specialized in animal portraits.[31]

WILLIAM MCVEY (b. 1905, Boston, Massachusetts–d. 1995, Cleveland, Ohio) attended Rice University in Houston in the late 1920s, then studied art at the Cleveland Institute of Art (1928). He also studied sculpture 1929–31 in Paris, France. He taught 1932–35 at the Cleveland Museum of Art, Cleveland College, and 1936–38 at the Museum of Fine Arts, Houston. He taught 1937–47 at the University of Texas at Austin. He served in the U.S. Army Air Corps at Randolph Field, San Antonio, during World War II. He was later stationed in the Philippine Islands. After the war, he taught at Ohio State University in Columbus and the Cranbrook Academy of Art in Michigan from 1942 to 1953. Subsequently, he headed the sculpture department of the Cleveland Institute of Art until he retired in 1967. The University of Texas School of Fine Arts created an endowed scholarship in his name. McVey's Texas works include the friezes on the San Jacinto Monument near Houston, the monument to James Bowie in Texarkana, the Davy Crockett monument at Ozona, and the sculptures on the grounds of the Texas Memorial Museum in Austin. His sculptures for the Section of Fine Arts include two reliefs (now lost) for the Houston post office—now a federal building—and two relief sculptures for the Littlefield, Texas, post office.[32]

JENNE MAGAFAN (b. 1916, Chicago–d. 1952, Albany, New York) grew up with her sister Ethel (also a painter and muralist) in Colorado. The sisters spent 1940–45 in California. Jenne studied at the Colorado Springs Fine Arts Center. Her teachers included Frank Mechau and Boardman Robinson. One of her mural designs for the Section of Fine Arts was selected in *Life* magazine's "48 States Competition." She exhibited widely throughout her career and won many prizes. Magafan completed murals for the Beverly Hills Hotel, the Social Security Building in Washington, D.C., and post offices at Glenwood Springs, Colorado (in collaboration with her husband Edward Chavez); Albion, New Mexico; Anson, Texas; and Helper, Utah. In 1945 she moved to Woodstock, New York, where she lived with her husband.[29]

FLETCHER MARTIN (*b. 1904, Palisades, Colorado–d. 1979, New York City*) left home at age sixteen, became a migrant worker for a year, then joined the U.S. Navy. Upon leaving the service, he earned his living as a printer. After several years, he moved to San Francisco where he took classes at the Stickney School of Art. While there, he joined the art cooperative classes of the Mexican muralist David Alfaro Siqueiros. Martin collaborated with Siqueiros on the mural for the San Pedro, California, federal building. From 1935 to 1940, he taught at the Art Center School in Los Angeles. He moved to New York City but soon left to take a one-year position as artist-in-residence at the University of Iowa, replacing Grant Wood. He later was appointed head of the painting department at Kansas City Art Institute. However, in 1943, he took a leave of absence when *Life* magazine hired him (along with several other artists) to illustrate the U.S. involvement in World War II. After the war, he lived in New York, then moved to Woodstock, New York, where he built a house.[30]

FRANK ALBERT MECHAU, JR. (*b. 1903, Wakeeney, Kansas–d. 1946, Denver, Colorado*) studied at University of Denver and then at the Art Institute of Chicago during the 1920s. After spending 1929–31 in Paris, France, he returned to Colorado, where he painted, taught, and created murals for the federal Public Works of Art Project and the Section

of Fine Arts. He taught for two years at Colorado Springs Fine Arts Center and was awarded a Guggenheim Fellowship in 1934. In addition to his murals in Texas, his work adorns the walls of the Denver Public Library, the U.S. Post Office in Washington, D.C., as well as post offices in Colorado Springs and Glenwood Springs, Colorado. His work is held in the collections of the Museum of Modern Art in New York and the Detroit Institute of Arts. He taught again at the Colorado Springs Fine Arts Center 1937–38 and next at Columbia University 1939–43. During World War II he worked as a *Life* magazine war correspondent.[33]

BARSE MILLER (*b. 1904, New York City–d. 1973, Mexico*) exhibited widely during his active career as a landscape painter, educator, and muralist. His work won numerous prizes in exhibitions in California and around the country. In 1946, he received a Guggenheim Fellowship. He completed a mural for the U.S. post office at Island Pond, Vermont, as well as murals for the Burbank, California, and Baytown, Texas, post offices. Miller served as chief of the Combat Art Section at General Douglas MacArthur's Pacific headquarters during World War II. He wrote several feature articles for *Life* and *Fortune* magazines. He also taught at Chouinard Art School, and held various other teaching positions. He was chair of the art department of Queens College, Flushing, New York, and served on the boards of various art councils.[34]

LOREN NORMAN MOZLEY (*b. 1905, Brookport, Illinois–d. 1989, Austin, Texas*) was a painter, graphic artist, lecturer, writer, and educator. He was reared and attended school in Albuquerque, New Mexico. In 1926, he moved to Taos to paint. He traveled Europe 1929–31, painting; he studied at the Academy Colarossi and the Académie de la Grande Chaumiere. He moved in the early 1930s to New York City, where he worked as a painter and earned a living as an engraver. He taught at the University of New Mexico 1936–37. Then, in 1938, he went to Austin, Texas, to help Ward Lockwood build the art department at the

University of Texas. He served as chair of the university's art department 1942–45 and again 1958–59. In the 1950s and '60s, he traveled to Latin America. He was a member of the Taos Art Academy and the Texas Fine Arts Academy. His work was exhibited in Colorado, at the Texas General Exhibition (1941–46), and annually in Dallas, Houston, San Antonio, among other locations. He received the Cokesbury prize, Dallas, 1943, and a prize from the San Antonio Art League, 1945. He completed murals for the Albuquerque federal building, and the U.S. post offices in Alvin, Texas, and Clinton, Oklahoma. His monograph on John Marin was published for the Marin Exhibit at the Museum of Modern Art in 1936. He taught in 1940 at the University of New Mexico; 1942–45 at the University of Texas; and at the University of Southern California during the summers of 1953 and 1954.[35]

PAUL NINAS (b. 1903, Cape Girardeau, Missouri–d. 1964, New Orleans), an abstractionist, studied at the University of Nebraska, then at Robert College in Constantinople and later at the Royal Academy, Vienna, and the Beaux Arts Academy in Paris. He traveled extensively in the Middle East, Mediterranean, and Caribbean. In 1930, he bought a coconut farm in the West Indies and painted colorful landscapes of his surroundings, later exhibiting them in New York City. In 1932 he moved to New Orleans, where he was appointed director of the New Orleans Art School and became a leader in the local art scene. His work is represented in many major museums.[36]

ALICE REYNOLDS (b. 1910, Albany, Texas–d. 1983, Albany, Texas) received her bachelor's degree in music from Baylor University then went on to graduate study in music at Sul Ross State University. She also studied painting with Xavier Gonzalez and Paul Ninas and developed as a painter and muralist. She exhibited her work at the Annual Allied Arts Exhibition in Dallas in 1929, and, in 1939, her mural design for the Robstown post office mural appeared in Life magazine's "48 States Competition" and was ex-

hibited at the Whitney Museum of American Art in New York. She also exhibited her paintings in Abilene, Fort Worth, Cape Cod, Sophie Newcomb College in New Orleans, and with the Art Students League of New York. She worked in New York as a commercial artist for several years. Continuing with her interests in music, she composed many tunes and was co-creator of the outdoor musical Fandangle after returning to Albany, where she also taught music in public schools.[37]

SUZANNE SCHEUER (b. 1898, San Jose, California–d. 1984, Santa Cruz, California) spent her early years in Holland but later returned to California to live on a fruit farm. In 1918 she studied briefly at the California School of Fine Arts, going on to four years of study at the California School of Arts and Crafts in Berkeley. She then traveled to Europe to work as a designer. She returned to the California School of Fine Arts where she studied fresco painting with Ray Boynton. She held teaching positions at Los Banos and Salinas public schools and for ten years at the College of the Pacific in Stockton, California, before moving to Santa Cruz, where she designed and built several houses. She completed work for the WPA and contributed to the mural decorations of Coit Tower in San Francisco under the Public Works of Art Project. She was living in retirement in Santa Cruz when she died.[38]

EUGENIE FREDERICA SHONNARD (b. 1886, Yonkers, New York–d. 1978, Santa Fe, New Mexico), a painter, sculptor, and craftsperson, studied at the New York School of Applied Design for Women and the Art Students League. She also studied with Auguste Rodin and Émile Bourdelle in Paris, France. She exhibited her work there and in New Mexico. Among the numerous prizes for her work was the grand prize at the 1940 New Mexico State Fair. In addition to the post office mural in Waco, Texas, her work adorns many public buildings in New Mexico. Her specialties included Pueblo Indians, furniture design and carving, and constructing iron bird cages.[39]

MAXWELL STARR (b. 1901, *Odessa, Russia–d. 1966, New York City*) studied at the National Academy of Design and New York University. A painter, sculptor, and teacher, he won numerous prizes in the 1920s. His murals include those in the U.S. Customs Office in New York; Brooklyn Technical High School; and the post offices in Rockdale, Texas, and Siler City, North Carolina. He held a teaching position with the Boys' Club of New York City in 1940 and went on to found the Maxwell Starr School of Art in New York City and East Gloucester, Massachusetts.[40]

THOMAS M. STELL, JR. (b. 1898, *Cuero, Texas– d. 1981, Dallas*) was a painter, muralist, graphic artist, and teacher who lived in Dallas, San Antonio, and Austin. He studied at Rice Institute in 1922 and received the Waterman Scholarship. He also studied 1923–25 at the Art Students League of New York with George Bridgemen, George Luks, and Charles Hawthorne. He worked as a set designer for Broadway plays and for films. From 1924 to 1928 he studied at the National Academy of Design in New York. Later, in 1931, he received his master of fine arts degree from Columbia University. He received two honorable mentions at the Prix de Rome Competition. He was a teacher at the Dallas Art Institute 1928–29 and in 1932. He instructed painting and drawing classes at the Dallas Architectural Club, served as artist and regional director for the WPA, and was a portrait painter. A member of the Dallas Artists League and Lone Star Printmakers, he exhibited at the 1933 Dallas Allied Artists exhibit and at the Texas State Fair Exhibition the same year. In 1939, his work was selected for *Life* magazine's "48 States Competition" that featured post office murals sponsored by the Section of Fine Arts. Stell completed murals for post offices in Longview and Teague, Texas, and Perry, Oklahoma. He also created other murals and mosaics in Corsicana, Dallas, and San Antonio. He taught at Trinity University 1942–43 and at the University of Texas in 1945.[41]

RAY S. STRONG (b. 1905, *Corvallis, Oregon–unknown*) studied at the California School of Fine Arts. As a land-scape painter and muralist, he was active in several art societies in the San Francisco area. Among his works are murals for the White House and the U.S. post offices in Decatur, Texas, and San Gabriel, California. In addition, he created dioramas for the 1935 California Pacific International Exposition in San Diego and held the position of diorama painter for the U.S. Forest Service 1935–38 and the National Park Service 1940–41. He also was educational director of a California art group.[42]

MINETTE TEICHMUELLER (b. 1871, *La Grange, Texas–d. 1970, Nacogdoches, Texas*) studied for a year at the Chicago Academy of Fine Art under Hugo D. Pohl, whom she married. She studied at Sam Houston Normal School and the San Antonio Academy of Art. She taught art in several Texas schools, including the San Antonio Academy of Art at the time she painted the mural in Smithville, Texas. She and her husband established an artist colony in Leon Springs.[43]

ALLIE VICTORIA TENNANT (b. 1892, *St. Louis, Missouri–d. 1971, Dallas*) spent most of her life in Dallas, where she attended public schools. She later attended the Art Students League of New York. A leading sculptor and member of the "Dallas 13" in the 1930s, she had studied at the Anspaugh Art School, Dallas, and with several sculptors, including George Bridgman, Edward McCartan, and Eugene Steinhof. She taught at the Dallas Art Institute and the Dallas Public Evening School. Her "Tejas Warrior," a nine-foot-tall bronze sculpture of a Tejas Indian warrior drawing his bow, was commissioned in 1936 for the Texas Hall of State Building in Fair Park, Dallas. In addition, she created several fountains and garden sculptures. Her work was widely exhibited and won many awards.[44]

THEODORE VAN SOELEN (b. 1890, *St. Paul, Minnesota–d. 1964, Santa Fe, New Mexico*) Van Soelen became a landscape and portrait painter after studying 1908–11 at the St. Paul Art Institute and 1911–15 at the Pennsylvania Academy of Fine Arts, where he won a travel scholarship to Europe. He painted winter landscapes along with other Pennsylvania impressionists. After contracting pneumonia and tuberculosis, he moved to Albuquerque, New Mexico, where he became a western landscape painter and illustrator. From 1922, he maintained two studios, one in Santa Fe and the other in Cornwall, Connecticut, becoming a permanent resident of Tesuque, New Mexico, in 1926. He exhibited widely, painting murals for federal arts projects in the Grant County Courthouse in Silver City, New Mexico, and the post offices at Portales, New Mexico, Waureka, Oklahoma, and Livingston, Texas.[45]

JOHN LAW WALKER (b. 1899, Glasgow, Scotland–unknown) moved to the United States and lived in Burbank, California. His teachers included Millard Sheets and Tolles Chamberlain. His critical success in the 1930s included earning a prize from the 1934 Southern California Festival of Allied Artists. He was forty years of age when he completed the Lockhart mural. Other murals include one for the Treasury Department building in Washington, D.C., and the Section of Fine Arts mural for the South Pasadena, California, post office. He taught at the Glendale (Arizona) Junior College in 1940 and was the recipient of many prizes.[46]

JULIUS WOELTZ (b. 1911, San Antonio–d. 1956, San Antonio), after studying under Wilson K. Nixon, José Arpa, and Xavier Gonzalez, studied for a year at the Académie Julian, Paris. He then studied at the Art Institute of Chicago and, later, independently in both Mexico and France. Returning to the United States, he taught in San Antonio, then joined Sul Ross State Teachers College in Alpine, becoming head of the art department there in 1932. He taught 1934–36 at the New Orleans Art School. When he received the Section of Fine Arts commission for the Amarillo post office mural panels, he moved to Amarillo. In 1941, he joined the art faculty of the University of Texas at Austin. He served in the U.S. Army Air Corps, stationed in San Antonio, during World War II. After the war he resumed his teaching at the University of Texas. He moved in 1951 to San Antonio for the last five years of his life. Woeltz exhibited his work in numerous shows in New Orleans and Chicago and throughout the states of California, New York, and Texas. In addition his post office murals in Amarillo and Elgin, Texas, he painted murals for public buildings in Alpine, Austin, Buda, Fort Worth, and San Antonio.[47]

BERNARD ZAKHEIM (b. 1898, Warsaw, Poland–d. 1985, San Francisco), a Polish refugee, settled in San Francisco in 1920 to practice his trade as an upholsterer. He also continued his study of art, which he began while he lived in Europe, at the Mark Hopkins Art Institute (later called the California School of Fine Arts and presently called the San Francisco Art Institute). He lived and worked in San Francisco and was one of several artists who, under the Public Works of Art Project, painted frescoes on the walls of the San Francisco landmark Coit Tower. He also painted the post office murals in Mineola (now destroyed) and Rusk, Texas. His murals also appear in the Alemany Health Center, the Jewish Community Center, the University of California Hospital, and the University of California Medical School, all in San Francisco.[48]

JAMES MILFORD ZORNES (b. 1908, Camargo, Oklahoma) studied with Millard Sheets during the mid-1930s and at the Otis Art Institute in 1938. He lived in Nipomo, California, and Mt. Carmel, Utah, his current residence, earning his living as a painter, designer, illustrator, and teacher. His preferred medium is watercolor. He has exhibited widely and won many prizes. He held teaching positions at various institutions, including the Otis Art Institute, 1938–46, and Polytechnic Junior High School in Pasadena, California, in 1940. After serving 1943–45 as an official artist in the U.S. Army, he taught 1946–50 at Pamona College and for a year at the University of California in Santa Barbara. In addition to the Section of Fine Arts mural in the El Campo, Texas, post office, Zornes painted a mural for the Claremont, California, post office.[49]

PHOTOGRAPHIC CREDITS

Unless otherwise indicated, all photographs are used with the permission of the Texas Historical Commission.

COLOR SECTION

Gwinn, Matt: Pages 108–109

Hyde, Scott: Pages 110–11

McSpadden, Wyatt: Pages 112–17, 120–36

Parisi, Philip: Pages 105–107, 118–19

BLACK AND WHITE PHOTOGRAPHS

Gwinn, Matt: Page 98

Hyde, Scott: Pages 27, 34, 64

McSpadden, Wyatt: Pages, 18, 22–23, 28–29, 36, 41, 47, 49, 53, 55, 56, 58–62, 65, 67, 71, 75–77, 82–83, 87, 89, 96, 100–101

National Archives, Section of Fine Arts, Public Building Administration: Pages, 19, 24, 38–39, 48, 63, 68, 79, 84–85, 92. Permission granted by National Archives.

Parisi, Philip: Pages 20, 25, 32–33, 35, 42–43, 46, 51–52, 69, 73–74, 78, 81, 88, 90, 91, 94, 99, 102–103

Smithsonian American Art Museum: Page 17. Permission granted by Smithsonian.

NOTES

PREFACE

1. John C. Carlisle, *Images Past and Present.*

2. *Texas Monthly,* "The Big Picture," Aug., 1989, pp. 94–103.

3. Philip Parisi, "People's Art: Finding Our Regional Roots in Depression-era Murals," *Dallas Life* magazine, *Dallas Morning News,* Sun., Nov. 4, 1990.

THE STORY OF TEXAS POST OFFICE MURALS

1. Some Texas mural sites have multiple murals.

2. Works Progress Administration (WPA); Civil Works Administration (CWA); Federal Emergency Relief Administration (FERA); Civilian Conservation Corps (CCC).

3. For a clear and concise summary of the motivations of federal support of the arts and the origins of the Section of Fine Arts and other New Deal art programs, see the introduction to the exhibition catalogue by Marlene Park and Gerald E. Markowitz, *New Deal for Art: The Government Art Projects of the 1930s with Examples from New York City & State.*

4. Diego Rivera, José Clemente Orozco, and David Alfaro Siqueiros also painted numerous murals in the United States, and their work became very popular in this country early in the 1930s. Matthew Baigell, *The American Scene: American Painting of the 1930s,* p. 41.

5. Quoted in Karal Ann Marling, *Wall-to-Wall America: A Cultural History of Post-Office Murals in the Great Depression,* p. 31.

6. Quoted in Robert E. Sherwood, *Roosevelt and Hopkins, An Intimate History,* p. 57. See also Marling, *Wall-to-Wall America,* p. 42.

7. Edward Bruce, head of the Public Works of Art Project, memorandum in support of a project to employ artists under Emergency Relief Appropriation Act of 1935, quoted in Marlene Park and Gerald Markowitz, *Democratic Vistas: Post Office Murals and Public Art in the New Deal,* n. 7, p. 31.

8. Richard D. McKinzie, *The New Deal for Artists,* p. 36.

9. Baigell, *The American Scene,* p. 46. PWAP art appeared in hospitals, schools, museums, libraries, and other public buildings. The artworks are difficult to trace because of poor record keeping. Many PWAP artworks have been destroyed or lost. The murals created for post offices, however, are the best documented of the federally supported programs of this era.

10. The WPA sponsored the Federal Art Project from 1935 to 1943 primarily to provide relief for artists, with the idea to reintegrate them as useful members of society by creating public artworks. Selection of particular artists for relief was made on the basis of financial need, not necessarily the quality of their work. Park and Markowitz, *New Deal for Art,* pp. 8–9.

11. Baigell, *The American Scene,* pp. 41–42.

12. See Park and Markowitz, *New Deal for Art,* pp. 26–29.

13. Edward Rowan, as chief administrator, served as an assistant under Edward Bruce, who held the position of Section of Fine Arts director.

14. Marling, *Wall-to-Wall America,* p. 21.

15. Ibid., p. 21.

16. Arthur M. Schlesinger, Jr., *The Politics of Upheaval,* vol. 3 of *The Age of Roosevelt,* p. 571.

17. Marling, *Wall-to-Wall America,* pp. 21–22.

18. For a more detailed discussion of this ballad, see Odessa entry.

19. Emil Bisttram, letter to Edward Rowan, chief administrator, Section of Fine Arts, Nov. 18, 1938, Records of the Public Building Service, Record Group 121, Inventory Entry 133, Box 107 (College

Park, Md.: National Archives and Records Administration). Hereafter NARA, RG 121, IE 133.

20. Bisttram to Rowan, Dec. 12, 1938, NARA, RG 121, IE 133, Box 107.

21. Tom Lea to Rowan, Nov. 14, 1940, NARA, RG 121, IE 133, Box 108.

22. Theodore Van Soelen to Rowan, May 7, 1940, NARA, RG 121, IE 133, Box 106.

23. Van Soelen to Rowan, Oct. 26, 1940, NARA, RG 121, IE 133, Box 106.

24. Van Soelen to Rowan, May 22, 1941, NARA, RG 121, IE 133, Box 106.

25. Van Soelen to Rowan, July 3, 1941, NARA, RG 121, IE 133, Box 106.

26. Merida Jaggers to author, July 21, 1992.

27. Several federal buildings containing Section of Fine Arts murals were transferred to the General Services Administration in 1949.

A GALLERY OF TEXAS POST OFFICE MURALS

1. The dimensions noted in this book are overall measurements and do not reflect the cutout for the postmaster's door that occurs in some murals.

2. "Post Office Mural Shows South Texas Panorama," *The Alice Echo*, June 22, 1939, NARA, RG 121, IE 133, Box 103.

3. H. B. Almond, Alice postmaster, letter to Carlie Saunders, volunteer coordinator for Texas Commission on the Arts, reply to TCA mural survey, Oct. 21, 1982. Letter on file with the U.S. Postal Service historian's office, Washington, D.C.; a copy in the author's possession.

4. Moya del Pino to Rowan, Nov. 28, 1935, NARA, RG 121, IE 133, Box 103.

5. Rowan to del Pino, Mar. 29, 1939, NARA, RG 121, IE 133, Box 103.

6. Del Pino to Rowan, Apr. 27, 1939, NARA, RG 121, IE 133, Box 103.

7. Cleo Congrady, member, Alvin Museum Society, telephone interview by author, June 16, 1994.

8. Loren Mozley to Rowan, Mar. 25, 1942, NARA, RG 121, IE 133, Box 103.

9. Rowan to Mozley, Apr. 1, 1942, NARA, RG 121, IE 133, Box 103.

10. "It May Be Art But —," *Time*, July 15, 1940, p. 50, NARA, RG 121, IE 133, Box 103.

11. Julius Woeltz to *Time*, July 11, 1940 (unpublished), NARA, RG 121, IE 133, Box 103.

12. Press release, Federal Works Agency, Public Buildings Administration, n.d., NARA, RG 121, IE 133, Box 103.

13. Ibid. Other regional competitions for post office murals in Texas included El Paso, 1937, and Dallas, 1938. Competing artists receiving Texas commissions were Bernard Arnest (Denver), Wellington; Jerry Bywaters (Dallas), Farmersville; Edward Chavez (Colorado Springs), Center; Xavier Gonzalez (New Orleans), Kilgore; Frank Mechau (Redstone, Colo.), Brownfield; Maxwell Starr (New York City), Rockdale; and Theodore Van Soelen (Santa Fe), Livingston.

14. "'Cowboy Dance' Mural Draws Caustic Comment," *The Observer* [Anson, Texas], n.d., NARA, RG 121, IE 133, Box 103.

15. Ibid.

16. *Bulletin of the North Texas Agricultural College* 13, no. 4 (June, 1930): 136. North Texas Agricultural College is now the University of Texas at Arlington.

17. Otis Dozier to Rowan, Nov. 7, 1940, NARA, RG 121, IE 133, Box 103.

18. A. C. Barnes, Arlington postmaster, letter to Rowan, June 9, 1941, NARA, RG 121, IE 133, Box 103.

19. This mural was completed for the Goose Creek, Texas, post office. Later, Goose Creek became part of Baytown.

20. Rowan to Barse Miller, Jan. 6, 1938, NARA, RG 121, IE 133, Box 103.

21. Peter Hurd to Rowan, n.d., NARA, RG 121, IE 133, Box 193.

22. Joe Pickle, "Reviewing the Big Spring Week," *Big Spring Daily Herald*, Sept. 12, 1937, NARA, RG 121, IE 133, Box 103.

23. Nat Schick to Rowan, Sept. 7, 1938, NARA, RG 121, IE 133, Box 103.

24. Rowan to Edward Bruce, July 5, 1938, NARA, RG 121, IE 133, Box 103.

25. Justice Harlan S. Stone, Edward Bruce MSS, 1939, Reel D89, Archives of American Art, quoted in Park and Markowitz, *Democratic Vistas*, p. 11.

26. Peter Hurd to wife Henriette Hurd, July 24, 1938, in Robert Metzger, ed., *My Land Is the Southwest: Peter Hurd, Letters and Journals.*

27. Ibid.

28. Hurd to Rowan, n.d., NARA, RG 121, IE 133, Box 103.

29. Ibid.

30. José Aceves, quoted in Mary W. Clarke, "José Aceves: Mexican Artist of El Paso Excels in Landscapes and Westerns," *The Cattleman*, Nov., 1955, NARA, RG 121, IE 133, Box 103.

31. Darlene White, "Mural from old post office now a fixture at museum," *Borger News-Herald*, June 14, 1991.

32. Ed Benz, director, Hutchinson County Museum, telephone interview by the author, Apr. 5, 1994.

33. "Artist Who Painted 'Longhorns' on Post Office Mural Has Never Seen a Longhorn," newspaper clipping, Apr., 1939, NARA, RG 121, IE 133, Box 103.

34. Gordon Grant to Rowan, Apr. 21, 1939, NARA, RG 121, IE 133, Box 103.

35. Grant to Rowan, Mar. 28, 1938, NARA, RG 121, IE 133, Box 103.

36. James Dallas, Brownfield postmaster, quoted in a letter from S. W. Purdum to W. E. Reynolds, commissioner of Public Buildings, Federal Works Agency, May 6, 1940, NARA, RG 121, IE 133, Box 103.

37. See Marling, *Wall-to-Wall America*, pp. 61–71 and 175–76, for discussions of mural controversies outside of Texas.

38. Rowan to Frank Mechau, May 15, 1940, NARA, RG 121, IE 133, Box 103.

39. Mechau to Rowan, May 17, 1940, NARA, RG 121, IE 133, Box 103.

40. Dallas to Rowan, May 21, 1940, NARA, RG 121, IE 133, Box 103.

41. Ibid.

42. Mechau to Dallas, May 29, 1940, NARA, RG 121, IE 133, Box 103.

43. Ibid.

44. Rowan to Mechau, May 29, 1940, NARA, RG 121, IE 133, Box 103.

45. Dallas to Mechau, Sept. 9, 1940, NARA, RG 121, IE 133, Box 103.

46. Dallas to Rowan, Oct. 5, 1940, NARA, RG 121, IE 133, Box 103.

47. "Mural in Place at Brownfield," *Fort Worth Star-Telegram*, Oct. 23, 1940, NARA, RG 121, IE 133, Box 103.

48. Dallas to Rowan, Dec. 4, 1940, NARA, RG 121, IE 133, Box 103.

49. Press release, Section of Fine Arts, Feb. 15, 1941, NARA, RG 121, IE 133, Box 103.

50. Ibid.

51. Gordon Huff to Inslee A. Hopper, consultant to the Section chief, May 2, 1940, NARA, RG 121, IE 133, Box 103.

52. Huff to Hopper, Mar. 19, 1941, NARA, RG 121, IE 133, Box 103.

53. Suzanne Scheuer, quoted in "Mural in Post office Attracts Much Attention," *The Caldwell News*, July 6, 1939, NARA, RG 121, IE 133, Box 103.

54. Ibid.

55. College Station postmaster, cited in John C. Carlisle, "Texas Post Office Mural Survey."

56. Dale McBee, Canyon postmaster, to author, Feb. 22, 1994.

57. Rowan to Edward Chavez, July 23, 1940, NARA, RG 121, IE 133, Box 103.

58. Ila McAfee to Rowan, Nov. 14, 1940, NARA, RG 121, IE 133, Box 103.

59. McAfee to Rowan, Jan. 8, 1941, NARA, RG 121, IE 133, Box 103.

60. McAfee to Rowan, Jan. 13, 1941, NARA, RG 121, IE 133, Box 103. J. Frank Dobie was a popular Texas folklorist who wrote a book on Longhorn legend.

61. McAfee to A. L. Bronstad, postmaster, Jan. 29, 1941, NARA, RG 121, IE 133, Box 103.

62. Rowan to Bronstad, Jan. 17, 1941, NARA, RG 121, IE 133, Box 103.

63. Bronstad to Rowan, May 29, 1941, NARA, RG 121, IE 133, Box 103.

64. "New Mural Painting In The Clifton Post Office," *Clifton* [Texas] *Record*, May 16, 1941, NARA, RG 121, IE 133, Box 103.

65. Rowan to Victor M. Arnautoff, Oct. 16, 1937, NARA, RG 121, IE 133, Box 103.

66. Arnautoff to Rowan, Sept. 27, 1937, NARA, RG 121, IE 133, Box 103.

67. Arnautoff to Rowan, Oct. 25, 1937, NARA, RG 121, IE 133, Box 103.

68. Rowan to Arnautoff, Oct. 4, 1938, NARA, RG 121, IE 133, Box 103.

69. Nicholas Lyon to Rowan, Aug. 24, 1938, NARA, RG 121, IE 133, Box 103.

70. Inslee A. Hopper, consultant to the Section chief, to Lyon, Sept. 2, 1937, NARA, RG 121, IE 133, Box 103.

71. Lyon to Rowan, Nov. 23, 1937, NARA, RG 121, IE 133, Box 103.

72. Rowan to Lyon, Mar. 15, 1938, NARA, RG 121, IE 133, Box 103.

73. Rowan to Lloyd Goff, July 12, 1938, NARA, RG 121, IE 133, Box 103.

74. Goff to Rowan, Jan. 5, 1939, NARA, RG 121, IE 133, Box 103.

75. Goff to Bruce, Nov. 27, 1939, Box 103.

76. Howard Cook to Rowan, July 12, 1940, NARA, RG 121, IE 133, Box 103.

77. Ibid.

78. Hurd to Rowan, Sept. 25, 1939, NARA, RG 121, IE 133, Box 104.

79. Ibid.

80. Artists to Rowan, Sept. 11, 1938 (Signed by Reveau Bassett, Charles T. Bowling, Jerry Bywaters, Harry Carnohan, John Doug-

lass, Otis Dozier, Alexandre Hogue, William Lester, Perry Nichols, Thomas Stell, Jr., Olin Travis, and Everett Spruce), NARA, RG 121, IE 133, Box 104.

81. Ibid.

82. Ibid.

83. Alexandre Hogue to Rowan, Nov. 4, 1937, NARA, RG 121, IE 133, Box 104.

84. Hatton W. Sumners, congressman, to Rowan, Sept. 9, 1937, NARA, RG 121, IE 133, Box 104.

85. Rowan to John William Rogers, drama editor, *Daily Times Herald* [Dallas, Texas], n.d., NARA, RG 121, IE 133, Box 104.

86. Edward Biberman to Rowan, Oct. 20, 1937, NARA, RG 121, IE 133, Box 104.

87. Ibid.

88. Rowan to Biberman, Oct. 25, 1937, NARA, RG 121, IE 133, Box 104.

89. Peter Hurd to wife Henriette Hurd, Jan. 20, 1940, in Metzger, ed., *My Land Is the Southwest.*

90. Hurd to Rowan, Jan. 22, 1940.

91. Hurd to Henriette Hurd, Jan. 24, 1940, in Metzger, ed., *My Land Is the Southwest.*

92. Hurd to Henriette Hurd, Feb. 3, 1940, in Metzger, ed., *My Land Is the Southwest.*

93. Hurd to Henriette Hurd, Feb. 21, 1940, in Metzger, ed., *My Land Is the Southwest.*

94. Ray Strong to Rowan, Nov. 18, 1938, NARA, RG 121, IE 133, Box 104.

95. Suzanne Scheuer to Forbes Watson, advisor, Section of Painting and Sculpture, Oct. 19, 1938, NARA, RG 121, IE 133, Box 104.

96. "Eastland Visitor Guide," Eastland, Texas: Chamber of Commerce, n.d.

97. Holden Lewis, Associated Press, "Rip-roaring tale 'toad' by folks from Central Texas," *Houston Chronicle*, Dec. 17, 1989.

98. "Eastland Visitor Guide."

99. Ward Lockwood to Rowan, June 14, 1939, NARA, RG 121, IE 133, Box 104.

100. Hopper to Bruce, June 16, 1941, NARA, RG 121, IE 133, Box 104.

101. Erin M. McAskill, Edinburg postmaster, to Section of Fine Arts, Mar. 26, 1940, NARA, RG 121, IE 133, Box 104.

102. Milford Zornes to Rowan, June 8, 1939, NARA, RG 121, IE 133, Box 104.

103. A. L. Lincecum, postmaster, to Rowan, Jan. 16, 1940, NARA, RG 121, IE 133, Box 104.

104. Ibid.

105. Thomas Kraycirik, "Now valuable P.O. mural cost $670 in 1939," *El Campo Leader-News*, Oct. 24, 1990, p. 1-D.

106. W. P. Slaton, postmaster, to Hopper, June 17, 1939, NARA, RG 121, IE 133, Box 104.

107. Press release, Section of Fine Arts, n.d., NARA, RG 121, IE 133, Box 104.

108. Woeltz to Forbes Watson, July 20, 1939, NARA, RG 121, IE 133, Box 104.

109. Press release, U.S. Treasury Department, Apr. 28, 1937, NARA, RG 121, IE 133, Box 104.

110. Lea to Rowan, Oct. 9, 1937, NARA, RG 121, IE 133, Box 104.

111. Ibid.

112. Ibid.

113. Ibid.

114. Lea to Rowan, May 15, 1937, NARA, RG 121, IE 133, Box 104.

115. Lea to Rowan, Oct. 9, 1937, NARA, RG 121, IE 133, Box 104.

116. Ibid.

117. Rowan to Lea, Apr. 26, 1937, NARA, RG 121, IE 133, Box 104.

118. Lea to Rowan, May 2, 1937, NARA, RG 121, IE 133, Box 104.

119. Rowan to Bywaters, Sept. 11, 1939, NARA, RG 121, IE 133, Box 104.

120. Robert S. McElvaine, *The Great Depression: America, 1929–1941*, pp. 215–18.

121. See a discussion of the Robin Hood concept and America's cultural values in the 1930s, Ibid., pp. 210–11.

122. Richard M. Dorson, *America in Legend*, pp. 137–38.

123. For a more detailed discussion of the heroes in Texas post office murals, see Philip Parisi, "Pioneers, Bad Men, Rangers, and Indians: Heroes in Texas Post Office Murals," in Nancy Beck Young, William D. Pederson, and Byron W. Daynes, eds., *Franklin D. Roosevelt and the Shaping of American Political Culture.*

124. Rowan to Dozier, Aug. 15, 1941, NARA, RG 121, IE 133, Box 104.

125. Rowan to Dozier, Sept. 30, 1941, NARA, RG 121, IE 133, Box 104.

126. Joe De Yong to Rowan, July 19,1938, NARA, RG 121, IE 133, Box 105.

127. Ibid.

128. De Yong to Rowan, Sept. 10, 1938, NARA, RG 121, IE 133, Box 105.

129. Dozier to Rowan, Aug. 5, 1938, NARA, RG 121, IE 133, Box 105.

130. Rowan to Dozier, Aug. 11, 1938, NARA, RG 121, IE 133, Box 105.

131. J. R. Folkes, postmaster, to Rowan, Dec. 15, 1938, NARA, RG 121, IE 133, Box 105.

132. Alexandre Hogue to Rowan, June 6, 1937, NARA, RG 121, IE 133, Box 105.

133. Rowan to Hogue, July 7, 1937, NARA, RG 121, IE 133, Box 105.

134. Rowan to Hogue, Dec. 6, 1937, NARA, RG 121, IE 133, Box 105.

135. Hogue to Rowan, Nov. 24, 1937, NARA, RG 121, IE 133, Box 105.

136. Ibid.

137. "New Hogue Mural To Have Showing First at Hockaday," *Dallas Morning News*, Feb. 1, 1939, NARA, RG 121, IE 133, Box 105.

138. "Muralist Decorates Post Office Walls with Pioneer Scene," *Hamilton County News*, May 29, 1942, NARA, RG 121, IE 133, Box 105.

139. "Texas Ranger Camp Brings Color and Atmosphere to Post Office," *Hamilton Herald Record*, May 29, 1942, NARA, RG 121, IE 133, Box 105.

140. Lockwood to Rowan, May 29, 1942, NARA, RG 121, IE 133, Box 105.

141. Ellen D. Kennedy, fine art conservator, "Conservation Report, Post Office Mural, Hamilton, Texas," Aug., 1991, p. 3. The deleterious effects of air-conditioning and heating issuing from ducts (now sealed off) blowing air directly on the mural and the variable climate of the lobby took a toll on the mural over the years. Attempts by an amateur to touch up the mural produced more damage that had to be reversed by the conservator, according to the report. Cleaning and in-painting were completed in 1991 by Ellen Kennedy, Kennedy & Associates Art Conservation, Houston. Copy of report in author's possession.

142. Postmaster, telephone interview with John C. Carlisle, in Carlisle, "Texas Post Office Murals Survey."

143. Rowan to Paul Ninas, Dec. 15, 1936, NARA, RG 121, IE 133, Box 105.

144. Ninas to Rowan, June 26, 1937, NARA, RG 121, IE 133, Box 105.

145. Ibid.

146. "Wood Carving Is Hung In Local Post Office," *Hereford Brand*, May 22, 1941, NARA, RG 121, IE 133, Box 105.

147. J. R. Lipscomb to Hopper, May 20, 1941, NARA, RG 121, IE 133, Box 105.

148. Enid Bell to Hopper, May 19, 1941, NARA, RG 121, IE 133, Box 105.

149. Hopper to Bell, May 27, 1941, NARA, RG 121, IE 133, Box 105.

150. Nolan Grady, former Hereford postmaster, telephone interview by author, Mar. 25, 1994.

151. Kay Peck, "Carving adds a whittle flair to post office," *Hereford Brand*, Sept. 3, 1989.

152. Grady, interview, Mar. 25, 1994.

153. The ship channel was completed in 1914.

154. Press release, Section of Fine Arts, n.d., NARA, RG 121, IE 133, Box 105.

155. Press release, Section of Fine Arts, "Mural Painting by Alexandre Hogue, Houston Ship Canal—Early History," n.d., NARA, RG 121, IE 133, Box 105.

156. Hogue to Rowan, July 8, 1941, NARA, RG 121, IE 133, Box 105.

157. Karen S. Haigler, "The Murals of Alexandre Hogue," master's thesis, Rice University, Houston, May, 1993, p. 64.

158. Mimi Crossley, "New Deal Art—Where Did It Go?" *The Houston Post*, Sun., Mar. 14, 1976.

159. Ibid.

160. In Texas, William McVey also created the frieze on the exterior base of the San Jacinto Monument and the sculpture on the grounds of the Texas Memorial Museum at the University of Texas at Austin.

161. McVey to Hopper, Nov. 15, 1939, NARA, RG 121, IE 133, Box 105.

162. Ibid.

163. Artists were expected to pay for their own materials out of the vouchers they received for their murals from the Section of Fine Arts. There was no separate allotment for materials or travel.

164. McVey to Hopper, Nov. 15, 1939, Box 105.

165. Hopper to McVey, Dec. 4, 1939, NARA, RG 121, IE 133, Box 105.

166. McVey to Hopper, Feb. 13, 1940, NARA, RG 121, IE 133, Box 105.

167. Alexander Levin to Watson, n.d., NARA, RG 121, IE 133, Box 106.

168. Margaret A. Dobson to Rowan, Aug. 6, 1938, NARA, RG 121, IE 133, Box 106.

169. Dobson to Rowan, July 11, 1938, NARA, RG 121, IE 133, Box 106.

170. Carlisle, "Texas Post Office Mural Survey," manuscript; Survey, U.S. Postal Service, Postal Historian's Office, Washington, D.C., 1989. The Kaufman Post Office where Margaret A. Dobson's mural was originally displayed is located at 30 West Mulberry Street.

171. The Section required all mural artists to submit a large format photograph of the completed work to Washington. The black-and-white photos are on file in the National Archives and Records Administration, Still Pictures Branch, College Park, Maryland.

172. Rowan to Charles Campbell, Nov. 23, 1938, NARA, RG 121, IE 133, Box 106.

173. Campbell to Rowan, Sept. 20, 1938, NARA, RG 121, IE 133, Box 106.

174. Ibid.

175. Rowan to Campbell, Sept. 27, 1938, NARA, RG 121, IE 133, Box 106.

176. Ibid.

177. The murals are peeling from the wall in places. The lobby is not climate-controlled, and high humidity and a deteriorating building place these murals in danger. Helen Houp, conservator, "Examination Report," Feb. 7, 1997, Perry Huston & Associates, Inc., Center for the Conservation of Art, Fort Worth.

178. Xavier Gonzalez to Rowan, Apr. 14, 1941, NARA, RG 121, IE 133, Box 106.

179. Ibid.

180. "Exploration Is Theme Of Murals Now Completed At Post office Here," Kilgore News Herald, May 14, 1941, NARA, RG 121, IE 133, Box 106.

181. Ibid.

182. Ibid.

183. Press release, Section of Fine Arts, "Mural Painting by Tom Lewis: 'Horses,'" 1939, NARA, RG 121, IE 133, Box 106. Copy also on file at the Texas Historical Commission.

184. Rowan to Lewis, Dec. 2, 1938, NARA, RG 121, IE 133, Box 106.

185. The U.S. Postal Service abandoned the old post office, located at North First and Houston Streets. The local school district purchased the building for use as a storage facility.

186. Fletcher Martin to Rowan, Dec. 12, 1939, NARA, RG 121, IE 133, Box 106.

187. Ibid.

188. Ibid.

189. Postmaster to Rowan, Jan 9, 1940, NARA, RG 121, IE 133, Box 106.

190. Hopper to Postmaster, Feb. 13, 1940, NARA, RG 121, IE 133, Box 106.

191. Ibid.

192. Ethel Edwards to Watson, May 1, 1940, NARA, RG 121, IE 133, Box 106.

193. Edwards to Rowan, Jan. 4, 1941, NARA, RG 121, IE 133, Box 106.

194. Ibid.

195. Ibid.

196. Rowan to Arnautoff, Apr. 19, 1939, NARA, RG 121, IE 133, Box 106.

197. Arnautoff to Rowan, Nov. 5, 1938, NARA, RG 121, IE 133, Box 106.

198. Postmaster to Section of Fine Arts, Sept. 19, 1939, NARA, RG 121, IE 133, Box 106.

199. Rowan to Arnautoff, Sept. 29, 1939, NARA, RG 121, IE 133, Box 106.

200. Rowan to Arnautoff, Apr. 19, 1939, NARA, RG 121, IE 133, Box 106.

201. "Sculptured Panels Installed In Littlefield Post Office," Lamb County Messenger, Aug. 12, 1948, NARA, RG 121, IE 133.

202. "They're Here But What Are They: New Murals Arrive for Lobby of P.O.," County-Wide News [Littlefield, Texas], June 3, 1948.

203. James T. Coleman to S. W. Purdum, fourth assistant postmaster general, Aug. 7, 1939, NARA, RG 121, IE 133, Box 106.

204. Coleman to Van Soelen, Apr. 24, 1940, NARA, RG 121, IE 133, Box 106.

205. Coleman to Van Soelen, May 7, 1940, NARA, RG 121, IE 133, Box 106.

206. Van Soelen to Rowan, May 23, 1940, NARA, RG 121, IE 133, Box 106.

207. Ibid.

208. Van Soelen to Rowan, Oct. 8, 1940, NARA, RG 121, IE 133, Box 106.

209. Van Soelen to Rowan, July 18, 1941, NARA, RG 121, IE 133, Box 106. The old Livingston post office is now owned by the city and used as the police department headquarters.

210. A. A. Storey to Rowan, Apr. 17, 1939, NARA, RG 121, IE 133, Box 107.

211. Marling, Wall-to-Wall America, p. 7.

212. José Aceves to Rowan, May 16, 1939, NARA, RG 121, IE 133, Box 107.

213. Postmaster, interview by John C. Carlisle, in Carlisle, "Texas Post Office Mural Survey."

214. "Post Office Mural Depicts Old Giving Way to New," Mineola Monitor, Aug. 11, 1938, NARA, RG 121, IE 133, Box 107.

215. S. Lankford to Rowan, Aug. 6, 1938, NARA, RG 121, IE 133, Box 107.

216. Sam Weitz to Zakheim, Aug. 9, 1938, NARA, RG 121, IE 133, Box 107.

217. E. N. Robinson to Superintendent of Painting and Sculpture, Treasury Department, Aug. 6, 1938, NARA, RG 121, IE 133, Box 107.

218. Unpublished survey results provided to author by Corporate Information Services (Washington, D.C.: U.S. Postal Services, 1992).

219. Xavier Gonzalez to Rowan, Jan. 2, 1942, NARA, RG 121, IE 133, Box 107.

220. Quoted in letter from Walter Myers, fourth assistant postmaster general, to W. E. Reynolds, commissioner of public buildings, Federal Works Agency, May 18, 1942, NARA, RG 121, IE 133, Box 107.

221. Rowan to Gonzalez, July 17, 1942, NARA, RG 121, IE 133, Box 107.

222. Lea to Rowan, June 6, 1940, NARA, RG 121, IE 133, Box 107.

223. Ibid.

224. Postmaster, Odessa, Tex., telephone interview by author, Oct., 1992.

225. Press release, Section of Fine Arts, 1938, NARA, RG 121, IE 133, Box 107.

226. Emil Bisttram to Rowan, Oct. 9, 1938, NARA, RG 121, IE 133, Box 107.

227. Bisttram to Rowan, Apr. 11, 1939, NARA, RG 121, IE 133, Box 107.

228. Rowan to Alice Reynolds, June 10, 1940, NARA, RG 121, IE 133, Box 107.

229. Marling, *Wall-to-Wall America*, p. 21.

230. The Section of Fine Arts awarded Starr's commission in 1943; he completed the mural in 1947 after returning from World War II armed service.

231. Maxwell Starr to Rowan, Feb. 23, 1943, NARA, RG 121, IE 133, Box 107.

232. The Rosenberg mural was removed during post office remodeling in 1966. Its current location is unknown; it is presumed destroyed. Kandy Taylor-Hille, "History of the Rosenberg Post Office," Historical Marker File (Austin: Texas Historical Commission, May, 1993), p. 11.

233. Ibid.

234. Dean Faucett to Rowan, July 9, 1940, NARA, RG 121, IE 133, Box 107.

235. Marling, *Wall-to-Wall America*, pp. 196–97.

236. Bernard Zakheim, "Background and Description of Rusk, Texas, Post Office Mural," typescript, n.d., NARA, RG 121, IE 133, Box 107.

237. Ibid.

238. Ibid.

239. Rowan to Zakheim, Oct. 13, 1938.

240. Ibid.

241. Ibid.

242. Rowan to Zakheim, Jan. 4, 1939.

243. Carey Williams to Rowan, Oct. 18, 1938.

244. Rowan to Williams, Nov. 3. 1938.

245. Ibid.

246. Not all artists who were invited to participate in the Section's competitions reacted favorably to the opportunity to paint public murals. Renowned artist Maynard Dixon, for example, dismissed the San Antonio job as a non-opportunity. Considering the architectural drawings for the courthouse, he balked at the marginal space allotted, "allowing no development of any large unified theme," he reasoned. Dixon seemed miffed that a large sum was offered to needy artists who were then asked to decorate a tiny space where "there is room for only fragmentary bits, joined perhaps by some background mass of color . . . ." Dixon, claiming to have higher interests for American art than petty personal motives for complaining to the Section, both complimented the Section for its efforts and criticized it for poor planning of architectural spaces for public artworks. Such inadequate spaces, he argued, do not really provide artists with the chance to "develop their ideas, forget personal preciousness, and make their work reach out beyond the petty necessity of cash to the people at large, for whom, in the last analysis, it is designed." Dixon, in a hand-written note to his typed letter, claimed to have read his remarks to artist friends, mostly members of the American Artists Congress, who encouraged him to send it. Maynard Dixon to Rowan, Feb. 25, 1937, NARA, RG 121, IE 133, Box 107. Rowan responded by agreeing with Dixon that architects should consult with artists in planning building decoration space, but that the Section was launched for buildings already planned and constructed, and that it was better to offer artists the opportunity to begin a national program while it was available than not. Rowan to Dixon, Mar. 3, 1937, NARA, RG 121, IE 133, Box 107.

247. On March 19, 1840, a band of sixty-five Comanches, including women and children, met in a courthouse with representatives of the Texas government to negotiate release of white hostages. Supported by soldiers, some Texans forced their way into the meeting in an attempt to coerce the Indians to release the hostages. A battle ensued in which seven whites and thirty-five Indians were killed and several people were wounded on both sides; twenty-seven Indian women and children were captured. When Comanches outside heard of the fray, three or four white hostages were turned over, but about thirteen were killed. Because of this blunder on the part of Texans, the war with the Comanche destroyed any trust by Indians of the Texas government and prolonged war. Jody Lynn Dickson Schilz, "Council House Fight," *Handbook of Texas Online* (Austin: Texas State Historical Association, 2000).

248. Howard Cook, typed sheets, n.d., NARA, RG 121, IE 133, Box 108.

249. Press release, Section of Fine Arts, no. 10-34, May 21, 1937, NARA, RG 121, IE 133, Box 108.

250. Bob John, "Last Friday," *The Wheel of Fortune* [Rotary Club of San Antonio] 27, no. 21 (Nov. 25, 1938), NARA, RG 121, IE 133, Box 108.

251. Newspaper clipping, *San Antonio Light*, n.d., no title, NARA, RG 121, IE 133, Box 108.

252. Cook, "Heard from the Scaffold," notes to Rowan, n.d., NARA, RG 121, IE 133, Box 108.

253. Ibid.

254. "Mural Painter Tells How It Is Done," *San Antonio Light*, Nov. 28, 1938, NARA, RG 121, IE 133, Box 108.

255. D. J. Quill to Rowan, June 12, 1939, NARA, RG 121, IE 133, Box 108.

256. Quoted in a letter from Walter Myers, fourth assistant postmaster general, to W. E. Reynolds, commissioner of Public Buildings, Federal Works Agency, Nov. 17, 1941, NARA, RG 121, IE 133, Box 108.

257. Rowan to Myers, Nov. 24,1941, NARA, RG 121, IE 133, Box 108.

258. Lea to Rowan, Sept. 15, 1941, NARA, RG 121, IE 133, Box 108.

259. Minette Teichmueller to Rowan, Mar. 21, 1939, NARA, RG 121, IE 133, Box 108.

260. Teichmueller, quoted in press release, Section of Fine Arts, PBA-FA-14, n.d., NARA, RG 121, IE 133, Box 108.

261. Rowan to Thomas Stell, Jan. 12, 1939, NARA, RG 121, IE 133, Box 108.

262. Rowan to Stell, May 5, 1939, NARA, RG 121, IE 133, Box 108.

263. Bywaters to Rowan, Oct. 19, 1941, Jerry Bywaters Collection of Southwestern Art, Southern Methodist University, Dallas, Texas.

264. Press release, Section of Fine Arts, "Lumber Manufacturing," 1942, NARA, RG 121, IE 133, Box 108.

265. Eugenie Shonnard to Rowan, July 10, 1939, NARA, RG 121, IE 133, Box 108.

266. *Waco Times Herald*, n.d., NARA, RG 121, IE 133, Box 108.

267. J. M. Pitillo to Hopper, consultant to the chief, Division of Fine Arts, Treasury Department, May 20, 1939, NARA, RG 121, IE 133, Box 108.

268. Bernard Arnest to Section of Fine Arts, May 1, 1940, NARA, RG 121, IE 133, Box 108.

269. Arnest to Rowan, Nov. 13, 1939, NARA, RG 121, IE 133, Box 108.

270. Rowan to Arnest, Dec. 1, 1939, NARA, RG 121, IE 133, Box 108.

271. Rowan to Arnest, Sept. 4, 1940, NARA, RG 121, IE 133, Box 108.

272. Ibid.

APPENDIX C. TEXAS POST OFFICE MURAL ARTISTS

1. John and Deborah Powers, *Texas Painters, Sculptors & Graphic Artists: A Biographical Dictionary of Artists in Texas before 1942*, p. 2.

2. Ibid., p. 12; "Mural Placed in New Post Office," *Canyon News*, Sept. 8, 1938, NARA, RG 121, IE 133.

3. Peter Hastings Falk, ed., *Who Was Who in American Art*, vol. 1, p. 133.

4. Virginia Mecklenburg, *The Public as Patron: A History of the Treasury Department Mural Program*, p. 25; Falk, ed., *Who Was Who in American Art*, vol. 1, p. 133.

5. Falk, ed., *Who Was Who in American Art*, vol. 1, p. 269; Kay Peck, "Carving adds a whittle flair to post office," *Hereford Brand*, n.d., Sept. 3, 1989 (clipping on file with the Deaf Smith County Historical Commission, Hereford, Texas); Bell to Mrs. Sears, Nov. 6, 1969 (letter on file with the Deaf Smith County Historical Commission, Hereford, Tex.).

6. Mecklenburg, *The Public as Patron*, pp. 32–33; *http://www.askart.com*.

7. Francine Carraro, "Williamson Gerald Bywaters," *The Handbook of Texas Online*, The Texas State Historical Association, (*http://www.tsha.utexas.edu/handbook/online*; Mecklenburg, *The Public as Patron*, p. 40; Paula Grauer and Michael Grauer, comps., *Dictionary of Texas Artists, 1800–1945*, p. 16; "Jerry Bywaters," U.S. General Services Administration Web Site (*http://w3.gsa.gov*); Powers, *Texas Painters, Sculptors & Graphic Artists*, p. 7475.

8. Falk, ed., *Who Was Who in American Art*, vol. 1, p. 533.

9. Ibid., p. 627.

10. Press release, Section of Fine Arts, no. 10–34, May 21, 1937, NARA, RG 121; U.S. General Services Administration internet site (*http://w3.gsa.gov*); Powers, *Texas Painters, Sculptors & Graphic Artists*, pp. 104–105.

11. Masha Zakheim Jewett, *Coit Tower, San Francisco: Its History and Art* (San Francisco: Volcano Press, 1983), p. 127.

12. Falk, ed., *Who Was Who in American Art*, vol. 1, p. 907.

13. Ibid., p. 927.

14. Rick Stewart, *Lone Star Regionalism: The Dallas Nine and Their Circle*, p. 164; Kendall Curlee, "Otis Dozier," *The New Handbook of Texas Online*, *http://www.tsha.utexas.edu*; Powers, *Texas Painters, Sculptors & Graphic Artists*, pp. 142–44.

15. Edwards, memorandum, to Watson, Oct. 18, 1939, NARA, RG 121; Powers, *Texas Painters, Sculptors & Graphic Artists*, pp. 154–55.

16. Falk, ed., *Who Was Who in American Art*, vol. 1, p. 1094; *http://www.askart.com*.

17. Ibid., vol. 2, p. 1310; Powers, *Texas Painters, Sculptors & Graphic Artists*, pp. 191–92; *http://www.askart.com*.

18. Mecklenburg, *The Public as Patron*, pp. 65–66; Powers, *Texas Painters, Sculptors & Graphic Artists*, pp. 196–97.

19. Falk, ed., *Who Was Who in American Art*, vol. 2, p. 1347; *http://www.askart.com*.

20. *The Handbook of Texas Online*, (Austin: The Texas State Historical Association), *http://www.tsha.utexas.edu/handbook*, 1999; U.S. General Services Administration web site, *http://www.gsa.gov*; Powers, *Texas Painters, Sculptors & Graphic Artists*, pp. 231–33.

21. *Who Was Who in American Art*, vol. 2, p. 1651.

22. Hunter died in a 1993 automobile accident. Powers, *Texas Painters, Sculptors & Graphic Artists*, p. 248.

23. U.S. General Services Administration web site, http://www.gsa.gov; Catalogue to Peter Hurd: Benefit Exhibition and Sale (Big Spring, Tex.: Friends of the Howard County Library), 1984; "Peter Hurd (1904–1984)," catalogue for the benefit exhibition (Big Spring, Tex.: Friends of the Howard County Library, 1984); *http://www.askart.com*.

24. U.S. General Services Administration web site, *http://www.gsa.gov*; Press Release, Section of Fine Arts, Apr. 25, 1937, NARA, RG 121, IE 133.

25. Levin to Watson, n.d., NARA, RG 121, IE 133.

26. Falk, ed., *Who Was Who in American Art*, vol. 2, p. 2018.

27. Charles C. Eldredge, *Ward Lockwood, 1894–1963* (Lawrence: University of Kansas Museum of Art, 1974); *New Handbook of Texas Online*; Mecklenburg, *The Public as Patron*, p. 82; Grauer and Grauer, *Dictionary of Texas Artists*, p. 59; Powers, *Texas Painters, Sculptors & Graphic Artists*, pp. 310–11.

28. Powers, *Texas Painters, Sculptors & Graphic Artists*, p. 83.

29. Falk, ed., *Who Was Who in American Art*, vol. 2, p. 2158; *http://www.askart.com*.

30. Falk, ed., *Who Was Who in American Art*, vol. 2, p. 2188; *http://www.askart.com*.

31. Dorothy B. Gilbert, ed., *Who's Who in American Art*, p. 382; *http://www.askart.com*.

32. Powers, *Texas Painters, Sculptors & Graphic Artists*, pp. 335–36.

33. U.S. General Services Administration internet site (*http://w3.gsa.gov*); Powers, *Texas Painters, Sculptors & Graphic Artists*, pp. 350.

34. Falk, ed., *Who Was Who in American Art*, vol. 2, p. 2274.

35. Ibid., p. 2355; Powers, *Texas Painters, Sculptors & Graphic Artists*, pp. 367–68.

36. Falk, ed., *Who Was Who in American Art*, vol. 2, p. 2428; *http://www.askart.com*; Le Mieux Galleries (*http://www.lemieuxgalleries.com*); Louisiana State Museum (*http://www.lsm.crt.la.us/painting/ninas*.

37. Powers, *Texas Painters, Sculptors & Graphic Artists*, p. 425; *Albany News*, May 28, 1983; *http://www.usgennet.org/usa/tx/county/shackleford/salliekingcloyd*.

38. Mecklenburg, *The Public as Patron*, p. 104; Jewett, *Coit Tower*, p. 128; *http://www.askart.com*; Edan Milton Hughes *http://www.edanhughes.com*.

39. Falk, ed., *Who Was Who in American Art*, vol. 2, p. 2919.

40. Ibid., p. 3146.

41. Falk, ed., *Who Was Who in American Art*, vol. 2, p. 3159; Powers, *Texas Painters, Sculptors & Graphic Artists*, p. 487.

42. Falk, ed., *Who Was Who in American Art*, vol. 2, p. 3206.

43. Ibid., vol. 3, p. 3625; Powers, *Texas Painters, Sculptors & Graphic Artists*, p. 509.

44. Falk, ed., *Who Was Who in American Art*, vol. 3, p. 3267; Powers, *Texas Painters, Sculptors & Graphic Artists*, p. 509.

45. Falk, ed., *Who Was Who in American Art*, vol. 3, p. 3393.

46. Section of Fine Arts, *Bulletin*, 1939, NARA, RG 121; *http://www.askart.com*.

47. Powers, *Texas Painters, Sculptors & Graphic Artists*, p. 560. Powers lists locations where Woeltz painted murals in these cities.

48. Jewett, *Coit Tower*, p. 130; Falk, ed., *Who Was Who in American Art*, vol. 3, p. 3676.

49. Falk, ed., *Who Was Who in American Art*, vol. 3, p. 3688.

BIBLIOGRAPHY

ARCHIVAL SOURCES

Of all the New Deal federal art programs, the Section of Fine Arts kept the most complete records of its activities. These records are held in the National Archives and Records Administration, College Park, Maryland, as part of the Records of the Public Building Administration. Much of the material concerning post office murals is in Case Files Concerning Embellishments of Federal Buildings, Record Group 121, Inventory Entry 133. The records are stored in numbered boxes arranged alphabetically by state. For example, files about Texas post office murals are found in boxes 103–108. Individual folders within each box contain material on specific murals, including a miscellany of original correspondence and carbon copies, press releases, canvas samples, artists' biographies, memoranda, and clippings regarding each mural. A description of the contents of these and other records about New Deal art programs is found in W. Lane Van Neste and Virgil E. Baugh, comps., *Preliminary Inventory of the Records of the Public Building Service (Record Group 121)* (Washington, D.C.: General Services Administration, 1958), pp. 28–41. The inventory is reprinted in Francis V. O'Connor, *Federal Support of the Visual Arts: The New Deal Then and Now* (Greenwich, Conn.: New York Graphic Society, Ltd., 1969), pp. 131–43. Photocopies of some of the correspondence used in this book were made by John C. Carlisle in 1982 and are kept at the Texas Historical Commission headquarters in Austin.

SOURCES CONSULTED

Baigell, Matthew. *The American Scene: American Painting of the 1930s.* New York: Praeger Publishers, 1974.

Beckham, Sue Bridwell. *Depression Post Office Murals and Southern Culture: A Gentle Reconstruction.* Baton Rouge: Louisiana State University Press, 1989.

Brown, Milton W. *American Painting from the Armory Show to the Depression.* Princeton: Princeton University Press, 1955.

Bruce, Edward. *Art in Federal Buildings: An Illustrated Record of the Treasury Department's New Program in Painting and Sculpture.* Washington, D.C.: Art in Federal Buildings, Inc., 1936.

———. "Implications of the Public Works of Art Project," *American Magazine of Art*, March, 1934. Reprinted in Barbara Rose, ed., *Readings in American Art, 1900–1975.* New York: Praeger Publishers, 1975, pp. 93–94.

———. "The Public's Reaction to Murals and Sculpture Executed under the Section of Fine Arts" [Memorandum, RG 121] College Park, Md.: National Archives and Records Administration, n.d.

Bulletin of the North Texas Agricultural College [Arlington] 13, no. 4 (June, 1930).

Bywaters, Jerry. "Contemporary American Artists," *Southwest Review* 23 (April, 1938): 297–306.

Carlisle, John C. *Images Past and Present.* Austin: Texas Historical Commission, 1982. Slides/Tape.

———. "Texas Post Office Mural Survey." Austin: Texas Historical Commission, 1982.

Carraro, Francine. *Jerry Bywaters: A Life in Art.* Austin: University of Texas Press, 1994.

"Case Files Concerning Embellishments of Federal Buildings," Record Group 121, Inventory Entry 133. College Park, Md.: National Archives and Records Administration.

Contreras, Belisario R. *Tradition and Innovation in New Deal Art.* Lewisburg: Bucknell University Press, 1983.

Crossley, Mimi. "New Deal Art: Where Did It Go?" *Houston Post*, March 14, 1976, p. 29.

Dorson, Richard M. *America in Legend.* New York: Pantheon Books, 1973.

Einaudi, Mario. *The Roosevelt Revolution*. New York: Harcourt, Brace and Company, 1959.

Eldridge, Charles C. *Ward Lockwood, 1894–1963*. Lawrence: University of Kansas Museum of Art, 1974.

Falk, Peter Hastings, ed. *Who Was Who in American Art, 1564–1975: 400 Years of Artists in America*. 3 vols. Madison, Conn.: Sound View Press, 1999.

Gilbert, Dorothy B., ed. *Who's Who in American Art*. New York: R. R. Boker Company, 1959.

Haigler, Karen S. "The Murals of Alexandre Hogue." Master's thesis, Rice University, Houston, May, 1993.

Jewett, Masha Zakheim. *Coit Tower, San Francisco: Its History and Art*. San Francisco: Volcano Press, 1983.

Jones, Alfred Haworth. "The Search for a Usable American Past in the New Deal Era," *American Quarterly* 23 (December, 1971): 710–24.

Kalfatovic, Martin R. *The New Deal Fine Arts Projects: A Bibliography, 1933–1992*. Metuchen, N.J.: The Scarecrow Press, Inc., 1994.

Long, Frank W. *Confessions of a Depression Muralist*. Columbia: University of Missouri Press, 1997.

Marling, Karal Ann. *Wall-to-Wall America: A Cultural History of Post-Office Murals in the Great Depression*. Minneapolis: University of Minnesota Press, 1992.

McElvaine, Robert S. *The Great Depression: America, 1929–1941*. New York: Time Books, 1993.

McKinzie, Richard D. *The New Deal for Artists*. Princeton: Princeton University Press, 1973.

Mecklenburg, Virginia. *The Public as Patron: A History of the Treasury Department Mural Program*. College Park, Md.: University of Maryland Department of Art, 1979.

Metzger, Robert, ed. *My Land Is the Southwest: Peter Hurd, Letters and Journals*. College Station: Texas A&M University Press, 1983.

O'Connor, Francis V. *Federal Support for the Visual Arts: The New Deal and Now*. Greenwich, Conn.: New York Graphic Society, Ltd., 1969.

———, ed. *The New Deal Art Projects: An Anthology of Memoirs*. Washington, D.C.: Smithsonian Institution Press, 1972.

Parisi, Philip. "People's Art: Finding Our Regional Roots in Depression-era Murals," *Dallas Life* magazine, *Dallas Morning News*, Sun., Nov. 4, 1990.

———. "Pioneers, Bad Men, Rangers, and Indians: Heroes in Texas Post Office Murals," in *Franklin D. Roosevelt and the Shaping of American Political Culture*, ed. by Nancy Beck Young, William D. Pederson, and Byron W. Daynes. Armonk, N.Y.: M. E. Sharpe, Inc., 2000.

Park, Marlene, and Gerald E. Markowitz. *Democratic Vistas: Post Office Murals and Public Art in the New Deal*. Philadelphia: Temple University Press, 1984.

———. *New Deal for Art: The Government Art Projects of the 1930s with Examples from New York City & State*. Hamilton, N.Y.: Gallery Association of New York State, Inc., 1977.

Phillips, Cabell. *From the Crash to the Blitz, 1920–1939*. New York: The Macmillan Company, 1969.

Powers, John and Deborah. *Texas Painters, Sculptors & Graphic Artists: A Biographical Dictionary of Artists in Texas before 1942*. Austin: Woodmont Books, 2000.

Randle, Mallory B. *Murals and Sculpture of the Public Works of Art Project and the Treasury Section in the Southwest*. Master's thesis, University of Texas at Austin, 1967.

Schlesinger, Arthur M., Jr. *The Politics of Upheaval*, vol. 3 of *The Age of Roosevelt*. American Heritage Library Edition. Boston: Houghton Mifflin Company, 1960.

Sherwood, Robert E. *Roosevelt and Hopkins, An Intimate History*. New York: Grosset and Dunlap, 1950.

Stewart, Rick. *Lone Star Regionalism: The Dallas Nine and Their Circle, 1928–1945*. Austin: Texas Monthly Press, 1985.

Van Neste, W. Lane, and Virgil E. Baugh, comps., "Preliminary Inventory of the Records of the Public Building Service (Record Group 121)," in Francis V. O'Connor, ed., *Federal Support for the Visual Arts: The New Deal and Now*. Greenwich, Conn.: New York Graphic Society, Ltd., 1969.

INDEX

ISBN 1-58544-231-3